BORDERLAND IN RETREAT

BORDERLAND IN RETREAT

From Spanish Louisiana to the Far Southwest

Abraham P. Nasatir

UNIVERSITY OF NEW MEXICO PRESS

Albuquerque

TO MY PARTNER IN LIFE, TEACHING, AND SCHOLARSHIP
IDA HIRSCH NASATIR
AND TO OUR STUDENTS WHO KEPT US YOUTHFUL AND
HUMAN

Preface

After a half century of research and writing on various aspects of Spanish Louisiana, I thought I should synthesize my life's work. Hence during the past two years I have attempted to summarize the results of my research in a series of essays relating to Spanish Louisiana. The result is the present work. In order to round out the picture, I thought it necessary to summarize the work of other scholars in the "frontier areas." None of the sections has been published previously. Chapter one was read as a paper at Louisiana State University and chapter three was read as a paper before the American Historical Association.

The purpose of these essays is to interpret the rivalry over, and gradual recession of, the frontiers from the Mississippi River to the Rocky Mountain area north of Santa Fe. Each section is a story in itself. But the continual recession of the frontiers and the consequent international aspects and diplomacy requires in each instance some repetition. I have tried to keep this repetitive material in line with the then shifting borderland. My chief purpose has been to have each essay cover a frontier or borderland, be complete in itself, and obviate the necessity of cross reference and footnotes.

The scene of emphasis shifted from the Mississippi to the Missouri River, to the hinterland; from New Orleans, St. Louis, and Prairie du Chien—the extreme northern perimeter of Spanish influence—to the interior and to Santa Fe. In the south it shifted from New Orleans and Natchitoches to Texas and New Mexico. It winds up centering around Santa Fe and extending up the Rocky Mountain ledge, thus rivaling both British and American interests.

My purpose has been to convey the idea of the shifting borderlands, and at the same time, to try to identify movements. In the overall picture of the interplay of events and of involvements of various sections of the frontier, all the "frontiers" were considered parts of the frontier of Spanish Louisiana. Except for a few instances, I have distinguished between international and interprovincial frontiers.

In general, I have omitted footnotes and specific citations as well as a complete bibliography. I have noted a few items in the form of books and basic printed sources at the end of the book. For those interested in working in the field I might mention F.B. Steck, *A Tentative Guide to Historical Materials on the Spanish Borderlands*, published in 1943 (Philadelphia: The Catholic Historical Society of Philadelphia) and recently reprinted (N.Y.: Burt Franklin, 1971); J.D.L. Holmes, *A Guide to Spanish Louisiana, 1762-1806* (New Orleans: By the author, 1970), and by the same author, "Interpretations and Trends in the Study of the Spanish Borderlands: The Old Southwest," which appeared in the *Southwestern Historical Quarterly* (74: 461-77); W.S. Coker and J.D.L. Holmes, "Sources for the History of the Spanish Borderlands," which appeared in E.D. Dibble and E.W. Newton, eds., *Spain and Her Rivals on the Gulf Coast* (Pensacola, Fla.: Department of State, Historical Pensacola Preservation, 1970); W.S. Coker, et al., "Research in the Spanish Borderlands," *Latin American Research Review* 7:3-94; John Francis Bannon, *Spanish Borderlands Frontier 1513-1821* (Albuquerque: University of New Mexico Press, 1974); and finally, John Francis McDermott, ed., *The Spanish in the Mississippi Valley 1762-1804* (Urbana: University of Illinois Press, 1974).

In preparing this manuscript I have had most helpful aid from my colleague, Professor Richard T. Ruetten, to whom I am indebted for his sage advice and counsel. I also wish to thank Father John Francis Bannon, S.J., retired confrère at St. Louis University. But the dedication really states to whom I am most indebted.

Contents

List of Maps

BORDERLAND IN RETREAT

Introduction and Definition:
The Frontiers of Spanish Louisiana

The vast expanse at midcontinental North America, known as Louisiana after being so christened by La Salle in 1682, has a fascinating history growing out of exploration, expansion, and international rivalries of the three colonial powers most intimately involved in the settlement and conquest of the northern half of the New World. The Spaniards started early, wended their way northward from Mexico and edged into the Mississippi Valley, spurred on by rumors of adventure and fabulous wealth, and stalled initially only by Indian opposition. The French spilled into the upper Mississippi Valley from the St. Lawrence and Great Lakes area; they also, in time, colonized northward from the coast of the Gulf of Mexico and the mouth of the great river. On the eastern seaboard of North America the English planted their colonies and gradually expanded westward toward midcontinent. Parrying the French in the interior of the continent (Louisiana stretched from the Rockies to the Appalachians), the Spanish and the English blocked French east-west lateral expansion. The decisive French and Indian Wars eliminated French competition in North America. In the division of spoils, England acquired everything east of the Mississippi River except New Orleans; and Spain, ostensibly everything west to the Rockies. An Anglo-Spanish Frontier ran down the middle of the Mississippi River, with Spain controlling the lands to the west and both sides of the mouth. Thus, the eastern frontiers of what by French donation in late 1762 became Spanish Louisiana were neatly drawn at the Mississippi, although Spain's reacquisition of the Floridas in 1783 temporarily destroyed the symmetrical boundary. The frontier line of 1763 between Spain and England was easily recognized, if not always honored. The western boundary—the Rocky Mountains—could have had the same virtue. But such was not the case. In the first place, the settled area of Spanish Louisiana never reached the Rocky Mountain area; and secondly, the lack of specific treaty boundaries made the shifting of borderlands extremely variable, often dependent upon the power and the interest of the moment.

Spanish Louisiana included the area from the Mississippi River westward, thus creating the first frontiers on the Mississippi River. Then the frontiers shifted with the entrance of the independent young republic of the United States, and the Americans created an Anglo-Spanish frontier on the Upper Mississippi. The imprecision of boundaries and the numerous frontier clashes—clashes not only of claims and counterclaims, but of competition for Indian allies and trade—obliterates any definite demarcation of the Anglo-Spanish frontier on the Upper Mississippi. That area, however, did contain a Spanish-American frontier of Spanish Louisiana above the Ohio, which tended to persist until the early 1800s. An Anglo-Spanish frontier which we can place did develop along the Upper Missouri. This merged into the tricornered frontier of Spanish Louisiana some time after the turn of the nineteenth century. But from the viewpoint of the Spaniards, who invariably looked upon Spanish Louisiana as a defense barrier, or buffer, to their more valuable Kingdom of New Spain, the centers of power were St. Louis in the north and New Orleans, along the Gulf of Mexico in the south. Therefore, from the standpoint of local, national, and international frontiers, Spanish Louisiana had at least six. First was the Louisiana-Texas frontier which existed until after the Louisiana Purchase. The Gulf Coast area was, however, of less importance before the turn of the nineteenth century. The second frontier lay along the Lower Mississippi, dividing English and Spanish territory, and later American and Spanish territory. The third followed the Upper Mississippi, and, from 1762 to 1800, was chiefly an Anglo-Spanish frontier. Fourth was the area along the Upper Missouri, an Anglo-Spanish frontier until the advent of the Americans. Fifth was the triangle formed by the area between St. Louis and Santa Fe, and back across (diagonally) Spanish Louisiana. The sixth and last combined the latter two frontiers into a Spanish-American frontier resulting from the French sale of Louisiana to the United States against the wishes, and to the fear, of Spain.

Thus Louisiana, purchased with boundaries undetermined by treaty, brought about numerous shifts in Spanish borderlands as well as repeated conflicts. The Spanish struggled to establish a western boundary in the south, a continuation of the old Louisiana-Texas frontier, and contested American activity in the territory stretching from about the Platte to the Missouri and Yellowstone rivers. In part this split frontier was due to imperfect geographical knowledge, and to the persistent belief that the western affluents of the Mississippi and Missouri rivers originated in the mountainous area just north of New Mexico. This territory was well within the claimed area of New Mexico, one of the Provincias Internas de Occidente that served as buffer for the Kingdom of New Spain. The defensive line for New Spain thus spread in a semicircle, reaching from New Mexico to between Los Adaes and Natchitoches on the Louisiana-Texas frontier. The Spanish hoped to protect their empire against the feared aggressive Anglos, all the way from the coast of the Gulf of Mexico to the headwaters of the Red, Arkansas, Platte, Missouri, and Yellowstone rivers. Therefore, during the period when the sixth, or last frontier of Spanish Louisiana was extant, the Spanish opposed American penetration of the Upper Missouri (including the Lewis and Clark expedition), as well as American attempts to gain Indian loyalty. Before the Louisiana Purchase, the Spanish had little fear of losing either territory or Indian friendship. After the sale, it was otherwise, and Spain's last efforts, with aid of her Indian allies, were futile attempts to ward off the Americans and English. In 1819, Spain and the United States signed the Adams-Onís Treaty (ratified in 1821). Simultaneously independence from Spain was secured in North America and the Republic of Mexico established. These two events wiped out Spanish Louisiana. The subsequent Mexican-American frontier, which in later years succumbed to the manifest destiny of an aggressive American nation moving relentlessly towards the natural boundaries of the Pacific Ocean, was created.

The term "Spanish Louisiana" is not entirely my own, although I have crusaded for its wider usage, so that today it is a well-established term, both in Spain and in the United States. I began this campaign to popularize the name "Spanish Louisiana" as a graduate student, in my masters thesis on "The Chouteaus and the Indian Trade of the West." In that study I also insisted on using the name "Spanish Illinois" to describe Upper Louisiana during Spanish rule. In my doctoral dissertation, "Trade and

Diplomacy in the Spanish Illinois Country.," and in all of my published work since, I have insisted upon "Spanish Illinois" to describe the general Illinois country west of the Mississippi, and to distinguish it from British or American Illinois Country.

Speaking of the frontiers of Spanish Louisiana prompts the question of the scope of my work. Since my graduate study days at the University of California, I have concentrated on frontier activity and development in the upper part of Spanish Louisiana, or the Mississippi Valley. Taking my marginal reference points as the Mississippi River, Natchitoches, and the Rocky Mountains, I have worked northward, pushing the northeastern frontier of Spanish activity into the western hemisphere. In the course of my research, I have delineated frontier areas, and in my presidential address to the Pacific Coast Branch of the American Historical Association I attempted an abbreviated synthesis under the title, "Shifting Borderlands," published in the *Pacific Historical Review* (February, 1965).

With regard to the frontiers of Spanish Louisiana, I have ferreted out materials in over half of the world, and have published some of the results of that research. I presented the frontiers along the lower and upper reaches of the Mississippi under the titles: *Spanish War Vessels on the Mississippi* and *Before Zebulon Montgomery Pike* (the latter is as yet unpublished). For the Upper Missouri I offered my study, *Before Lewis and Clark*. The "Genesis of the Santa Fe Trail" and the midperiod border on the western side were partly covered, in collaboration with my former colleague and coauthor, the late Noel Loomis, in our study *Pedro Vial and the Roads to Santa Fe*. I am now in the process of completing a monograph on the last frontier of Spanish Louisiana, which will deal with the defense of the frontier against the onrushing Americans after 1804. That frontier extended along the eastern border of the Rockies north of New Mexico to the Yellowstone and Upper Missouri rivers. The study will end with Spain's expulsion from the North American continent in 1821.

With respect to the early frontier of Spanish Louisiana on the Lower Mississippi, I have done little original research. Distinguished historians have preceded me, and I have looked to their publications for aid and inspiration in presenting some of the material here. The same holds true for the frontier of Spanish Louisiana along the Gulf Coast, more commonly referred to as the

Louisiana-Texas frontier, where the scholarship has been equally outstanding.

However, with respect to all of the shifting borders of Spanish Louisiana on the Upper Missouri and Upper Mississippi, and north from New Mexico, I have relied exclusively upon my own research and upon documents gathered over the years, only a few of which have been published.

1

The First Frontier:
Along the Mississippi (to 1777)

Spain occupied her share of Louisiana reluctantly. France had ceded the province to Spain in November 1762, but not until May 1765, did the Spanish King appoint and commission Antonio de Ulloa as governor. By royal decree Ulloa was placed directly under the Ministry of State rather than under the Ministry of the Indies; Louisiana was to be governed according to its former laws and institutions insofar as practical. Ulloa arrived in March 1766 with a force of probably no more than ninety men. Effective occupation depended on inducing French troops stationed in Louisiana to enlist in the Spanish service. Most, however, refused when not offered pay equal to that of Spanish soldiers. Ulloa immediately told the Marqués de Grimaldi, Charles III's first Secretary of State, to raise French soldiers' pay to the Spanish standard, which he did; but even that failed to gain the desired enlistments. Spain got off to a shaky start in her new province.

Until his military forces could be augmented, Ulloa decided that it would be impossible to take full possession of Louisiana. A temporary expedient was adopted under which Charles Philipe de Aubry, formerly French governor and military commander, would govern as Ulloa's agent, while Spain assumed colonial expenses. This was the famous *"toma de posesión,"* and for a year and a half a governmental arrangement without precedent prevailed in the eighteenth-century Spanish empire. At Balize, a post near the mouth of the Mississippi, Ulloa signed with Aubry a tentative agreement for division of authority in the colony. This was to be effective until sufficient Spanish troops to ensure control arrived. As a symbol of the transfer, although Ulloa undoubtedly hoped that it was more than symbolism, the French flag at Balize was lowered and the Spanish colors raised in its stead. Ulloa was operating under trying circumstances, seeking to impress everyone, particularly the hostile New Orleans merchants, with power he did not in fact possess. Before his arrival, Ulloa notified the Superior Council in New Orleans of his appointment, but they gave him a frigid reception. For the previous two years the merchants and population of New Orleans had been in effective sovereign control, having been on their own, without aid, advice, or law from either France or Spain. The Frenchmen, then, were quite naturally apprehensive, and indeed, opposition to Spanish rule (as it later turned out to be) predominated in New Orleans upon Ulloa's arrival.

Ulloa, irked by the cool reception, refused to show his orders to the Superior Council, which may have fostered the belief that the transfer of Louisiana was not a permanent arrangement between France and Spain. In the face of strong resistance to Spanish control, stemming in part from the period of "salutary neglect," Ulloa could do little more than avoid clashes that might result in open rebellion. Without manpower to reenforce his government, his position was a mockery. He spent, consequently, barely a third of his time in New Orleans during his first year and a half as governor.

Soon after his initial trouble with the merchants, Ulloa left with Aubry to inspect the settlements, not returning to New Orleans until May 17, 1766. He started up the Mississippi but soon swung westward, overland, to Natchitoches. Distance and lack of time compelled him to abandon a trip to the northern posts in Illinois. When he returned, troubles began to increase. He withdrew supervision of the slave trade from the Superior Council and entrusted it to a board of his own selection. Matters became critical for Ulloa when, on orders from Spain, he directed Aubry to proclaim new commercial regulations. Although they were designed to protect the general public from profiteering, the merchants and shippers made violent objections. A decree of May 6, 1766, opened up limited trade with other Spanish colonies. Another, dated September 6, 1766, tightened control over importation of goods by English and French merchants in order to cut down on contraband and to encourage the development of native trade. So vigorous was the protest against the latter, which interfered with lucrative smuggling, that Ulloa was forced to suspend the edict for a while. Ulloa then withdrew to Balize where he established his headquarters until the following summer. Governmental affairs in New Orleans were left in the hands of Juan Joseph de Loyola, commissary of war and military intendant; Esteban Gayarré, contador, or royal comptroller; and Martín Navarro, treasurer.

One of Ulloa's chief objectives in Louisiana was to found new forts and settlements along the Mississippi as defenses against British settlements on the east bank. While at Balize, Ulloa laid the groundwork for fulfilling his goals. Expeditions were sent out: Lieutenant Juan Orieta founded San Gabriel in the Iberville district; Lieutenant Pedro Piernas established San Luis de Natchez on the west side of the Mississippi (about a league from British Natchez); Captain Francisco Ríu went to the mouth of the Missouri River where he built a fort on the south bank and a blockhouse on the north. Ulloa himself supervised the construction of a new establishment at the mouth of the Mississippi. He decided to abandon French Balize and build Isla Real Católica de San Carlos; to watch and oversee this, his personal pride and joy, Ulloa stayed at Balize, making it his headquarters in September 1766, and remaining there through the fall and winter.* Then Ulloa moved his permanent headquarters to Isla Real. There he married his Peruvian Princess fiancée. He had no love for New Orleans.

With widely dispersed establishments to supply and both French and Spanish governmental expenses to be met, Ulloa was soon pressed for funds. His expenses exceeded the annual allotment of 150,000 pesos, and the King approved an increase to 250,000 to become effective in January 1768. But additional funds came slowly and in insufficient installments. By 1766 the finances of Louisiana were already in dire straits. The accumulated shortages and debts inherited from the former government created a condition of insolvency. The last half of Ulloa's administration was characterized by a series of financial crises, and most of his correspondence consisted of appeals and pleas for men and money. Without both, Spanish control over Louisiana could not be maintained. Ulloa was forced to buy on credit; then had difficulty in meeting the government's obligations thus incurred. Soldiers and civilian employees frequently went unpaid. Spanish coins were disappearing, and French paper money, in which the French were speculating, could not be redeemed by Ulloa.

Promotion of foreign and domestic trade was imperative, if

Louisiana was to become financially independent of Spain. To expand the volume of trade, Ulloa had to confront two problems: the existence of large-scale smuggling with the British (especially at Natchez, and Fort Manchac about 115 miles above New Orleans); and the lack of a sound basis for a complementary trade with Spain.

French dissatisfaction with Spanish occupation was focused upon the person of the governor. By character and education Ulloa was not a man who appealed to inhabitants of a frontier community. He was an outstanding scientist, but taking notes on climate, geography, flora, and fauna seemed useless to most Frenchmen in New Orleans. And his King did not provide Ulloa with enough money or men to win the allegiance of the colonists. The cold reception of Ulloa had offended him. The more he saw of New Orleans and its inhabitants, the more contemptuous he became. The creoles reacted in kind, and were not inclined to listen to his promises. Yet, as an administrator Ulloa was sincerely interested in the welfare of the colony and did carry out his instructions as thoroughly as his limited resources permitted. In matters of general policy few changes were made during subsequent administrations.

Ulloa, treating the Indians as another facet of the problem of defense, adopted the French system of managing them. He utilized the services of experienced French commandants in the frontier posts, continued the French practice of giving the Indians presents, and depended upon licensed traders to keep the tribes under control. Notwithstanding the economic advantages which the English traders enjoyed, the French had cultivated the friendship of many Indian tribes on both sides of the Mississippi. The French method, emphasizing the trader and annual presents, differed radically from the Spanish mission-presidio system. And the Indians, too, were different from those whom the Spaniards had known. Everything was done to attract the Indians to their new master. During Ulloa and Aubry's tour to Natchitoches, conferences were held with the Indians, trade possibilities and sites for forts considered, and potential communication lines with Texas and New Mexico investigated.

The Indian trade was an extensive business and an important part of the provincial economy. Principal trade centers were St. Louis, Arkansas Post, and Natchitoches. In the Illinois country, Indian tribes from far away and from both sides of the Mississippi

Map 1—The Mississippi Basin before 1777

visited, traded, and received presents at St. Louis. From Natchitoches, traders and presents went out to various tribes. Governor Hugo O'Conor, of Spanish Texas, attempted to exclude Louisiana traders from his jurisdiction—but Ulloa regarded the trade as essential to the control of the Indians. After some difficulties with the Yatasi, Ulloa permitted Balthazar de Villiers, Spanish commandant at Natchitoches, to allow French traders to operate freely among the tribes of the Louisiana-Texas frontier. Captain Ríu in Spanish Illinois likewise made concessions to the traders in order to maintain better relations with them and with the Indian tribes that they served.

Immigration and colonization policy consumed a good deal of Ulloa's time and attention. With a larger population, Louisiana might become a permanent bastion against English aggressiveness. Despite the years of French effort, in 1776 there were only between five and six thousand inhabitants; no more than nineteen hundred were capable of bearing arms. Immigration was an obvious means of bolstering the population. In contrast to Spain's other colonies, foreign immigrants were welcomed in Louisiana. This was due in part to the fact that Spanish nationals refrained from entering Louisiana in large numbers because there were greater economic opportunities in other parts of the empire. Such colonization was to be an important element in the history of the entire Spanish period.

Upon his arrival, Ulloa found an Acadian migration already under way. He assisted these French refugees through gifts of land, agricultural implements, rations, and even livestock. The Acadians settled along the Mississippi River above New Orleans. To distribute the newcomers over a greater area, Ulloa ordered the last entering group to settle at San Luis de Natchez. This led to Acadian denunciation of the Spaniards for interference with their plans to settle in a single stretch of territory.

In the north, British occupation of Illinois and Canada persuaded many French inhabitants to move to the west side of the Mississippi. St. Louis, founded originally in February 1764, as a trading post by Pierre Laclède Liguest and Auguste Chouteau, quickly grew into a village of importance and was selected as the capital of upper Louisiana, or Spanish Illinois. Ironically, then, the greatest French settlement of Louisiana took place during Spanish rule. Acadian immigration alone continued for more than twenty years. Influenced by reports from Acadian friends, a number of Maryland Catholics opened negotiations with Ulloa for the purpose of obtaining permission to settle in Louisiana. The governor was agreeable and allowed representatives of their group to visit the province and to examine lands which might be suitable for the colonists.

Despite the lack of military force, Ulloa gave as much attention as possible to the problem of defense. The English "menace" was apparently foremost in his mind. The governor sought to prevent English traders from entering Spanish territory and dealing with the Indians. He closely watched British establishments along the eastern shores of the Mississippi and made recommendations concerning military defense.

During Ulloa's administration there was much unrest in the English colonies as well as in his own. The conduct and motives of the Louisiana merchants and shippers were not unlike those of New Englanders, and the Superior Council in New Orleans sought to maintain its authority as did Anglo colonial legislatures. But Spanish Louisiana had the additional problem of French discontent. Indeed, in the fall of 1768, the French organized a conspiracy to expel the Spanish from Louisiana. Led by those who had opposed Ulloa from the beginning, mainly merchants and landowners drawn from the upper class and the Superior Council, they opposed mercantile restrictions, and disliked Ulloa personally and Spanish rule in general. The Revolution, remarkably secret for a conspiracy (or was it a French family affair?) succeeded in reaching its objectives immediately, albeit in the long run temporarily. The events of the "Revolution of 1768" were executed quickly. On October 28 a demonstration was held by the Acadian and German settlers who came to drink wine (in effect, they were ordered to do so by the French leaders of New Orleans). The next day the Superior Council passed resolutions demanding the governor's banishment, and appealed to Louis XV to reclaim the colony. Lacking troops to resist, Ulloa and his family sailed down the river on November 1, and shortly thereafter from Balize for Cuba and Spain.

Spain's failure to supply troops, an unpropitious political and social environment in the colony accentuated by a myopic, mistaken policy developed in Madrid, inadequate financing, and Ulloa's refusal to show his commission to the Superior Council, all contributed to French rebellion against Spain and Ulloa. There were other reasons as well: longstanding Anglo-French rivalry on the Louisiana-Texas frontier, the nonredemption of French paper money, interference with free trade and smuggling, and the devious method of ruling through Aubry. An economic crisis in the summer of 1768 was the actual prelude to the rebellion, and Ulloa, well aware of what was happening, had not only forewarned his superiors, but had attempted to shorten red tape by appealing directly to the Viceroy of New Spain for help. As discontent mounted, Ulloa had kept Spanish Secretary of State Grimaldi informed. The conspiracy thus represented the culmination of two years of increasing opposition stemming from many factors, not the least of which was the aforementioned interregnum between French and Spanish rule, during which Louisiana citizens, virtually on their own, had developed a sense of independence incompatible with Spanish paternalistic rule.

In New Orleans a period of uneasy quiet followed the expulsion of Ulloa. Although the Spaniards who remained in Louisiana were not bothered, some of the troops were forced out. Local Spanish officials were retained, most likely because the Spanish government had debts and official presence encouraged the possibility of receiving some payment. Aubry, who had opposed the rebellion, exercised some restraining influence upon the inhabitants, and the fire of rebellion gradually subsided. The conspirators, however, devised a scheme to create a republic. They sought aid from the British, but were coldly received. And instead of popular support, they met opposition.

Aubry, as the nominal head of the colony after the departure of Ulloa, had the backing of several French conservatives and some soldiers. Although a few flareups occurred, general support for the defiance of Spain waned. In spite of the rebellion Spain did maintain ties and contacts, sending financial support to Joseph de Loyola, presents for the Indians, and succor for the French troops. Spanish rule in Upper Louisiana—Spanish Illinois—had not been disturbed. The insurrection had died after the first slogan—"Get the Spaniards out"—was enunciated, and before the latter part of the slogan—"establish French independence or the Old King"—had a chance to be instituted. It was not therefore a full revolution and never affected the rest of Louisiana.

In the meantime, Spain was considering possible courses of action. The Council of the Indies discussed alternatives after Ulloa's reports and full accounts were received. Spain could forget

Louisiana and leave it alone, or vindicate her honor by punishing the rebels. The case was thoroughly discussed, and the cost of maintenance of Louisiana was reviewed. Spain, however, realized the usefulness of Louisiana as a barrier against the English and decided to reestablish Spanish rule in Louisiana. National interest more than national honor determined the decision.

To implement this decision and to indicate seriousness of purpose, Spain placed Lieutenant-general Alejandro O'Reilly, distinguished military man of Irish ancestry, at the head of two thousand troops. He was the direct opposite of Ulloa, the Andalusian-born professor. O'Reilly's orders were simply to establish Spanish rule in Louisiana once and for all. The task did not appear overly formidable, for French Louisiana at best could have mustered only eighteen hundred soldiers.

O'Reilly sailed into the Mississippi and disembarked at New Orleans on August 18, 1769, taking possession of the province with great ceremony and little opposition. Three days later he arrested the leaders of the rebellion, and on August 26 he required all inhabitants to pledge allegiance to the King of Spain. Twelve rebel leaders were tried for treason. Five were condemned to death and six to prison terms of from six years to life. The twelfth died mysteriously in prison before the end of the trial. The property of all the leaders was confiscated.

In summary fashion O'Reilly established Spanish rule and stamped out the effects, if not the memory of, revolution; for this he has been branded in history as "Bloody O'Reilly." But he was much more than that. Even before the end of the trial, O'Reilly began a constructive and statesmanlike program. He turned attention to the political and economic reorganization of Louisiana. He mollified the French creoles and won their loyalty for Spain. He sought to bring prosperity and contentment to the Louisianians (instituting several welfare measures), and profit to the Spanish King. To further this dual program, he worked to prevent English encroachments onto Spanish soil, to exclude them from commerce in Lower Louisiana, to forestall instrusions in the Spanish Illinois and Arkansas regions, and to head off English aggression (caused by undue Spanish activity) east of the Mississippi. Whenever possible O'Reilly followed orthodox administrative patterns of the Spanish empire. But whenever particular conditions made French methods more suitable than Spanish, he adopted the former.

To prevent inflation, O'Reilly decreed price controls on food. He expelled undesirable merchants and enforced Spanish commercial regulations. He proposed and won approval for free trade between Louisiana, Havana, and ports of Spain. He abolished the Superior Council, created a cabildo, promulgated new laws and regulations, and reduced governmental expenses. He devised a plan of defense based on the organization of a strong colonial militia. He drew from the French population to fill many colonial offices. He placed effective administration under lieutenant-governors at Natchitoches and at St. Louis. To the first, he appointed the experienced Frenchman Athanase de Mézières who was to be responsible for securing the Louisiana-Texas frontier. To the second, veteran Spanish officer Pedro Piernas was sent as the first lieutenant-governor of Spanish Illinois. He appointed the local knowledgeable Frenchman, Louis St. Ange de Bellerive, to aid Piernas.

O'Reilly's Indian policy, in practice, paralleled Ulloa's. He used Frenchmen, French methods, and French policies. He assigned de Mézières the task of reconciling the Indians to the new regime, which the latter did quite effectively by making numerous journeys to the Indians, negotiating treaties with them, and supplanting unauthorized traders with licensed ones.

In Upper Louisiana the Indian problem differed slightly. Here and there were many friendly tribes, on both banks of the Mississippi, who hated the British. While Spain wanted to trade with the friendly tribes, she did not want to provoke the English into aggressive action. Although presents were given to the tribes east of the Mississippi, they were directed not to offend the English, nor to interfere with their navigation of the Mississippi. From St. Louis north, everything pertaining to the Indians was under the jurisdiction of the lieutenant-governor, who licensed traders, gave or withheld presents, and held councils. English traders were denied access to Spanish territory, and theoretically at least, there was to be no communication with them. For control purposes, a small garrison was located at or near the mouth of the Arkansas River, an entry point for English contraband trade. The problems of peace with (and the safety of) the Indians, and the security of the settlements were rendered more difficult by the intrusion of British traders from both West Florida and Illinois into the Indian country west of the Mississippi. Furthermore, English merchants along the Mississippi supplied unlicensed French traders with goods and thus diverted a good deal of commerce from legitimate Spanish channels. O'Reilly took severe measures to prevent this illegal trade, but as long as the English remained on the Mississippi it never entirely ceased.

O'Reilly investigated the condition of the posts established by Ulloa and decided that none was well located, either for military or economic purposes. He moved the headquarters of the river pilots back to the old French site of Balize, abandoned San Luis de Natchez, and turned over San Gabriel de Iberville on the lower Mississippi to German settlers in the area. On the Missouri he left only a few men to guard the mouth, and moved the garrison to St. Louis and Ste. Geneviève south of St. Louis.

If Louisiana was to be a barrier, it was plainly necessary to stop, or at least to slow down, the English at the Mississippi. O'Reilly therefore prohibited entry by English traders and settlers into Louisiana as well as commercial intercourse across the Mississippi. As noted above, he constructed forts along the river and created a citizen militia. Overall, his strategy was not to establish Louisiana as an impregnable bulwark against the English; simply to delay their advance.

O'Reilly made the transition to Spanish rule as painless as possible. His Code O'Reilly was a substantial abridgement of the *Recopilación de Leyes de los Reynos de las Indias* which, together with the French Black Code, was declared the law of the colony. Probably his most dramatic innovation was in commerce, although here too, he was not so much establishing new aspects of mercantilism as he was enforcing long-standing rules, aimed at a policy of exclusion. O'Reilly succeeded far better than had Ulloa because he had sufficient soldiers to command respect for mercantilism. The fear of contraband trade with Mexico from Natchitoches and Opelousas prompted O'Reilly to recommend frequent change of these post officials, so that they would not have time to become corrupted by illicit gains. He expelled some merchants, whom he suspected of contraband activities, from New Orleans. He acknowledged the right of the English to navigate the Mississippi but utilized all legal channels in an attempt to prevent them from navigating through Spanish territory to Manchac and Natchez.

By March 1770, O'Reilly believed that he had completed his task of reorganization, and as special commissioner of the King, he installed Luis de Unzaga y Amezaga as governor, and departed for Havana. The King expressed satisfaction with O'Reilly's work and approved his acts and recommendations. As a result of O'Reilly's occupancy, Louisiana became a dependency of the Captaincy General of Cuba and supervision of its affairs fell to the Ministry of the Indies. Spanish Louisiana was firmly under control.

Unzaga, by the mildness and restraint which characterized his administration, did much to reconcile French inhabitants to the Spanish regime. At the same time he continued O'Reilly's policies. Expansion of agriculture and trade, and population growth, took place. Unlike O'Reilly, however, Unzaga made little effort to check the contraband trade carried on between the inhabitants and the English, perhaps in large measure because of Louisiana's need for goods. English interest in the area led to increased commercial activities, the addition of floating stores on the Mississippi, and increased supplies for Louisiana planters.

During 1770 and 1771 there was a brief war scare stemming from the Falkland Islands dispute between Spain and England. The British commandants, Thomas Gage in New York and Sir Frederick Haldimand in Florida, laid plans for attacking Louisiana in case of war. Luis de Unzaga reported the presence of English reinforcements in Pensacola. From Havana, O'Reilly recommended sending one hundred men and supplies to Louisiana, which was done, and Unzaga was instructed to defend Louisiana as best he could. If attacked by a strong force, however, he was to retreat to Mexico. The detachment at Arkansas was similarly slated to withdraw, to Natchitoches, if necessary, and the Illinois troops were to seek shelter with friendly Indian tribes along the Missouri. Although General Gage was ordered to mobilize an army to attack Louisiana, no attack occurred; no war broke out.

The situation along the Louisiana-Texas frontier became difficult because of Spanish policy. Spain placed Louisiana under the jurisdiction of Havana, while Texas continued as part of New Spain. Different systems of Indian control were in vogue in the two regions. This led to conflict of policy on both sides of that border. Juan María Vicencio de Riperdá, the governor of Texas, did his best to cooperate with Louisiana authorities, relying upon them for the protection of Texas from the Indian "Nations of the North." Such cooperation, however, made Riperdá questionable in the eyes of the officials of New Spain, where the Louisiana policy was not approved.

Difficulties along the Louisiana-Texas frontier became as serious as an international problem, even though both provinces were part of the same Spanish empire. Nations of the North received presents from Natchitoches where de Mézières was lieutenant-governor. Natchitoches traders in turn purchased horses and mules from the Taovaya, who sold them to contraband traders from Arkansas, a profitable business that encouraged horsestealing from Spanish establishments. The Baron de Riperdá saw the advantages of the French methods and supported de Mézières. But Riperdá's superior forbade trade with, and furnishing arms to, the Indians. Therefore, the influence of French traders from Louisiana surpassed that of Spanish traders in Texas. The Spaniards of Texas could not oust the Indians though, for the latter would have gone over to the English.

Frontier forts and Indian policies did not succeed in keeping all English out of Louisiana after all. The advance wave of the Anglos crossed the Mississippi long before the American Revolution. In addition, Englishmen entered Spanish territory by way of the Gulf Coast or went across Louisiana to various parts of the Texas frontier. By 1769, four Englishmen were living at Natchitoches; by 1772 English firearms were found among the Taovaya Indians on the upper Red River.

The most troublesome problem in the Mississippi frontier area was that posed by the pugnacious Osage Indians, who disturbed peace and progress in Spanish Illinois and areas beyond. Osage depredations were widespread and destructive and included numerous attacks upon the French of the Arkansas and Natchitoches districts. Spanish control of the Osage was the responsibility of St. Louis officials, and Piernas quickly ordered a suspension of all trade with the Osage in order to bring them to heel. The trade embargo *seemed* logical, but traders from British Illinois recognized an opportunity. Jean Marie Ducharme obtained a trading license from the English and led a party to take over the trade of the Osage and Missouri Indians. In turn Piernas organized an expedition of volunteers who captured the supplies of the intercepted intruders. This did not stop British traders or completely cure the Osage problem. The Indians knew that they could trade with the enemies and rivals of the Spaniards; they also knew that certain Spanish traders in the Arkansas and Natchitoches districts would continue trade despite Spanish regulation and without license. The repentance of the Osage, which came as often as they were restricted effectively, was always temporary, and then only in proportion to their current supply needs.

The most portentous event of Luis de Unzaga y Amezaga's regime was the outbreak of the American Revolutionary War and the arrival of Anglo-Americans at the Mississippi. The English settlements on the east bank, especially those in the Natchez and Manchac districts, were growing faster than the settlements in Spanish Louisiana. Unzaga saw the Americans and British as a menace to Spanish control west of the river, fearing commerce in peace and armies in war. With the outbreak of the Revolutionary War, Unzaga's anxiety turned to alarm. Ordered to survey the situation, Unzaga concluded that Louisiana was in shaky military condition; if attacked, he would follow the advice of 1770 and fall back to Mexico.

The actual war forced Unzaga to face the problems of remaining neutral. Various revolutionary leaders importuned Unzaga to lend assistance to the revolutionary *bostoneses*. Unzaga was uneasy about Louisiana's vulnerability to attack, but he was not convinced that the surest defense was through aiding the Americans. Largely through the efforts and influence of Oliver Pollock, an Irish-American merchant in New Orleans, the first direct assistance from Spain to Americans did come under Unzaga's regime.

Although Unzaga begged to be retired, he was promoted to the Captaincy General of Caracas. He relinquished his office in New Orleans on January 1, 1777, and departed in March. He was succeeded by young Bernardo de Gálvez who, with the approval of the Spanish court, actively aided the Americans while strengthening provincial defenses. He seized English contraband vessels on the Mississippi and in 1777 ordered all English subjects to leave Louisiana. When Patrick Henry and Thomas Jefferson asked that New Orleans be made a free port for western American products, and that Americans be allowed to navigate the Mississippi River, Gálvez balked. He did not have the authority to change Spain's commercial regulations. Spain, taking all this into account, attempted to improve Louisiana's economic conditions by liberalizing commerce and expanding agriculture. In addition, restrictions on the Negro slave trade were somewhat relaxed.

With youthful and forceful Bernardo de Gálvez in charge of Spanish Louisiana, and with the entrance of Spain into the Revolutionary War, conditions on the frontiers of Spanish Louisiana changed, both for the better and for the worse. Spain recovered the Floridas, but the readjustment of borders and new alignments created more fears and problems. This new frontier of Spanish Louisiana, new certainly from the standpoint of a realignment of "foes," would bring additional stresses and strains to the Spanish empire.

2

The American Revolution and After:
The Frontier along the Mississippi

I

The American Revolution triggered a series of events that intensified British and Spanish rivalry in the Mississippi Valley. Spain saw a chance to regain the Floridas, lost to the English in the Seven Years War, as well as an opportunity to control the entire Mississippi basin. The ambitious Spaniards clearly sought certain economic advantages: the products of the back country of an independent neighbor could be shipped to, and exported from, New Orleans. If Spain regained possession of the Floridas, she would enjoy this trade. On August 15, 1777, the Spanish government informed Bernardo de Gálvez that, should the American rebels seize any of the British settlements on the Mississippi, and should they be disposed to deliver them up to the Spanish Sovereign, he (Gálvez) was empowered to receive them in trust or deposit, taking care not to provoke any countermeasures from England.

The American Revolution that broke out in 1775 did not involve all of England's provinces east of the Mississippi, for only the thirteen seaboard colonies took up arms. The Floridas, Canada, and the Mississippi-Ohio Valley remained loyal to England and these constituted the Anglo-Spanish frontier. At the outset, then, there was no change in the Anglo-Spanish frontier along the Mississippi as far south as Manchac. During the American Revolution, Louisiana was opened to the Americans on account of Spain's hostility toward England. American activities in the trans-Appalachia area, together with British and American activities in the lower portions of Louisiana, brought the American Revolution nearer to the Spanish frontier long before Spain entered that war. Two areas, Upper and Lower Louisiana, both British and

Spanish, were affected by the hostilities of the *bostoneses* against the British, with Indians involved on both sides.

The American colonies had revolted while Luis de Unzaga was still governor of Louisiana, and Unzaga, cautious, conservative, and lacking specific instructions, was rather lukewarm in his pro-Americanism. Spain took a lively interest in the American Revolution and Louisiana officials were directed to submit detailed and frequent reports of whatever echoes of the struggle reached them. Even so, Spain's policy remained undefined, and Unzaga was in a quandary about how he ought to treat the various Tories and Rebels with whom he came in contact. In all probability he would have followed a policy of strict neutrality, had it not been for Oliver Pollock. Pollock, a friend of Alejandro O'Reilly, who introduced him to Unzaga, was fluent in Spanish, a familiar figure in New Orleans, and from the outset an ardent partisan of the *bostoneses.* He served and suffered for their cause. (Pollock's diplomatic and financial assistance were important factors in American successes in the west.)

Thus the Spanish aided the Americans very early in their struggle for independence. As soon as 1776, Pollock (as agent for Virginia) attempted to enlist aid for the American cause from the Spanish at New Orleans. Exploiting his influence with Unzaga, he secured large quantities of gunpowder, which were sent to Forts Henry and Pitt, and to Philadelphia, thus marking the beginning of direct Spanish aid to the Americans. On April 18, 1777, the young, impetuous, and vigorously pro-American Bernardo de Gálvez, who had succeeded Unzaga on January 1, 1777, seized British vessels and ordered English subjects to leave Louisiana (in contrast to Unzaga, who had winked at English smuggling on the Mississippi). As a result English contraband trade with Louisiana was almost extinguished before Spain entered the war in 1779. Both Gálvez and Lieutenant-governor Fernando de Leyba of St. Louis, actively, though surreptitiously, aided the Americans. The high point of Gálvez' direct support of the Americans was his assistance to James Willing, who headed an expedition against British West Florida. Willing raided Loyalist settlements along the Lower Mississippi in February 1778, and was warmly welcomed in New Orleans. There he was commissioned to bring letters to New Orleans, supplies up the river, and to raid English settlements and seize vessels on the Mississippi. Willing's second task, to invade West Florida, met with disaster. His initial actions had led the British to reinforce West Florida and blockade the river. But by early 1778 the British flag was excluded from the Mississippi, with the Spanish in complete possession of its commerce. Gálvez recognized the dangers of war to Louisiana and saw in the American Revolution an opportunity to harass the English by giving direct assistance to their foes. He facilitated American shipping by sea and up the Mississippi, and cooperated with Pollock to send supplies to Washington's army and the army in the West. He was ordered to encourage the Americans to conquer the British posts near Louisiana. Spain also used secret agents as an intelligence service, as for example sending Jacinto Panis to Mobile and Pensacola. English officials vigorously protested these actions, particularly Spanish aid to the Americans and Spanish harassment of English activities. Their protests were more than verbal, for the English fired on boats descending the Mississippi from Illinois and had troops and Indians at Barrancas de Margot, near present Memphis. Spain, for her part, protested the presence of English traders among Indians west of the Mississippi. In effect, Gálvez seconded anything, short of war, in aid of Americans.

Gálvez also tried to strengthen Louisiana by means of increased immigration. He authorized de Leyba to grant inducements to Catholic settlers (especially French and Germans from British-held territory east of the Mississippi) to settle in Spanish territory. He imported Canary Islanders and colonists from Málaga. Many pro-Americans also fled to Spanish Louisiana. One group of immigrants founded Galveztown.

The conquest of British Illinois by American George Rogers Clark in 1778-1779 brought the war to the very doorstep of St. Louis, capital of Spanish Illinois. Clark wrote Patrick Henry in 1777 that possession of Kaskaskia would guarantee control of the Ohio and Mississippi rivers, insure steady supplies from the Spanish, and increase trade with the Indians. In the long run, however, trade suffered, and the way was prepared for British commercial monopoly, extended by the merchants of Michilimackinac, after the Revolutionary War.

Meanwhile, in the north, Lieutenant-governor Fernando de Leyba who had been appointed on March 9, 1778, was ordered to encourage immigration into Spanish Illinois, to treat all British and American émigrés in Spanish territory with fairness and in accord with the rights of Spanish subjects, and to engage in secret correspondence with the Americans. He was to listen for rumors of war strategies in the British area directed against the Spanish power and colonies. He was to secure the friendship not only of the Indians within the dominions of Spain, but also of those under British jurisdiction. And he was to do all this without implicating the Spanish government and without inviting British complaints and reprisals.

De Leyba did aid the Americans, and Clark in particular. Twenty-six days after taking office, he engaged in a long and very friendly correspondence with Clark. He invited Clark to visit St. Louis, where de Leyba welcomed him with great ceremony. An intimate relationship between the two developed, and the Americans benefitted correspondingly. Supplies were obtained from merchants in St. Louis and New Orleans, and Clark's success was, in great part, due to Spanish aid and supplies. When the credit of the Americans fell, de Leyba backed purchases from St. Louis merchants with his own funds. Spain's aid was not inconsiderable, and yet anxious for the friendship of the Indians in its territory and the security of its possessions, Spain naturally spent much more on Indian presents than on aid to the Clark campaign across the river. The Spaniards gave more than financial help to the Americans, however. To avoid British destruction of American supplies on the Mississippi, Pollock's supplies were shipped under the Spanish flag and consigned to de Leyba; thus, the ships were able to slip past the British post at Natchez. Without this ruse it would hardly have been possible for Clark to hold the country he had conquered. In addition Clark was helped by Joseph Maná Francesca (Francisco) Vigo, a business associate of de Leyba; by Gabriel Cerré, a French Canadian by birth, a British subject by virtue of his residence and business in Kaskaskia, but Spanish in sympathy; by Charles Gratiot; and by Father Pierre Gibault, another Canadian. Louis Perrault of St. Louis acted similarly for the British.

De Leyba, whose traders had seized the goods of two English counterparts, watched the British movements closely. He told Gálvez that Fort Carlos III located at the entrance of the Missouri River was useless and suggested the establishment of forts at Aguas Frias just north of St. Louis and at the mouth of the Des Moines River. These were to be garrisoned with a strong force to prevent Englishmen from using that river by which they had already penetrated Spanish territory as far as the Missouri . Gálvez informed de Leyba that he could not sponsor such an ambitious program because of the expense, at least not without authorization of the court. But he did instruct the lieutenant-governor to prevent incursions of English traders and the enticement of "our Indians."

The British, too, were active. Almost from the outset they were aware of Spanish aid to the Americans. In October 1776, Sir Guy Carlton, then British governor of North America, wrote Lieutenant-governor Henry Hamilton in Detroit, telling him to intercept correspondence between the Spaniards and Americans but to take care not to create a breach between England and Spain. "The Spanish side must be respected upon all occasions," Carlton warned. The English intended to drive the rebels out of Illinois in order to cut off their communication with the French and Spanish. They were alarmed when the Spaniards wanted to erect forts in the Illinois country, and they worked to defeat Spanish attempts to win native support. Indeed, Hamilton wrote Gálvez on January 13, 1779, requesting him to prohibit New Orleans commerce in gunpowder with the rebels. Hamilton also warned Gálvez that if rebels took refuge in Spanish territory to avoid a British force he would be obliged to attack the Spanish posts. And just eleven days later, he informed General Frederick Haldimand of his belief that war existed with both France and Spain, but that he had received no word to justify offensive action.

The British traders, as noted, had entered Spanish territory and were trading along the Des Moines River. They attempted to plant a post at the mouth of the Ohio; and they attempted to take over the mouth of the Missouri where they could undersell the Spaniards and control the Indians. They hoped that Hamilton's reconquest of Vincennes from Clark would permit realization of these ambitions. When Hamilton accomplished that feat, he communicated to Pensacola his plans for a joint attack upon the Americans in the West. But Francisco Vigo gave the plans to Clark, and the latter reconquered Vincennes and captured Hamilton. In these important events, Clark, aided by the creoles in Illinois, relied chiefly on Pollock and Gálvez for essential supplies. From Vincennes Hamilton summed up his view of the combatants: "The Spaniards are feeble and hated by the French, the French are fickle and have no man of capacity to advise or lead them, the Rebels are enterprizing and brave, but want resources, and the Indians can have their resources, but from the English, if we act without loss of time in the favorable conjuncture." Such was the British attitude in the year preceding Spain's declaration of war upon England, an attitude that persisted until war broke out with Spain, when attempts were made to bring British plans to fruition.

In June 1779, Spain severed relations with England, and on July 8, declared war, ordering her colonies to attack British possessions. England, on the other hand, interpreted Spain's initial severance of relations as a virtual declaration of war. Lord George Germaine wrote General Haldimand on June 17 that Spain had declared war, and he told Haldimand to commence hostilities. Orders were given to attack New Orleans and reduce the Spanish posts in the Illinois.

During the winter and spring of 1780, the British made comprehensive plans to conquer the West and cut off east-west communications, thereby freeing men for duty on the Atlantic seaboard. They planned to enlist the Indians to join British troops coming up the Mississippi, surprising the Spanish forts and capturing exposed parties, settlements, and villages. In preparation for this ambitious program and in order to meet similar activities on the part of the Spaniards, the British stationed spies and merchants among the Indians of the Illinois. Planning for the capture of Upper Louisiana was left to British Governor Patrick Sinclair at Michilimackinac, who proceeded with energy and dispatch. The Spanish province was coveted not only because of its wealth of furs, but also because its capture was part of an extensive movement to encircle the rebellious American colonies, cut off their supplies via the Mississippi and Ohio rivers, and open the way for British attacks and Indian forays in the west. Sinclair immediately took steps to win the allegiance and aid of the Sioux under chief Wabasha, and of the Sac and Fox Indians.

British strategy included four simultaneous movements. Captain Charles Michel de Langlade would attack from Chicago all along the Illinois River; another party would watch Vincennes; Wabasha and the Sioux who accompanied the main party attacking St. Louis (under Emmanuel Hesse) would attack the rebels at Kaskaskia and Ste. Geneviève. Traders who joined Hesse's expedition were to be recompensed by getting exclusive rights to the Missouri trade. Captain Henry Bird would "amuse" Clark at the Falls of the Ohio while an expedition under General John Campbell would proceed from Mobile up to the Mississippi. The expeditions from the north and the south would join at Natchez.

The first important objective of this potent force was the capture of St. Louis, which the British hoped would guarantee control of the rich fur trade in the Missouri Valley. But even more important, the strategic location of St. Louis made its occupation essential to any successful control or defense of the Mississippi Valley. The British assumed that St. Louis was vulnerable because of the carelessness of the inhabitants and because of its weak defenses, both in men and cannon. Since that was the primary object of the British move from the north, the other expeditions, such as of that of Langlade, were to serve as rear guards. To distract the Americans still further, Bird was to stage his raids, and the expedition including Pottawatami Indians was planned against Vincennes. This was the most comprehensive movement for the conquest of the West that the British undertook during the Revolution, and one that appeared to have every guarantee of success.

When Spain entered the war, Gálvez received orders to conquer Pensacola, Mobile, and the British posts on the Mississippi. The Spaniards also feared a British attack on New Orleans. But Gálvez had long anticipated a British attack as well as the Spanish Crown's desire to regain the Floridas. He prepared well. He learned of British plans to attack the Mississippi colonies of Spain, to reinforce Natchez, Baton Rouge, and Manchac with fifteen hundred Canadians, and to dispatch an equally large expedition by sea from Pensacola. Gálvez kept news of the Spanish declaration of war on England secret while formulating defense plans. In fact, even his own soldiers were unaware that war had been declared until the first actual attack. He believed that Louisiana's best defense was an attack on the British posts on the Mississippi. He therefore struck at Baton Rouge, Manchac, and Natchez, conquering four hundred and eighty leagues of fertile Lower Mississippi land, and driving the English from the banks of the Mississippi River. He then proceeded to conquer Mobile and Pensacola, and wrested the Floridas from English hands. Meanwhile, Balthazar de Villiers, a Frenchman in Spanish service and commandant of Arkansas Post, crossed the Mississippi River. On November 22, 1780, he took formal possesion of the east bank of the Mississippi, north of Natchez, in the name of Spain.

Map 2—The Mississippi Basin after 1777

The other part of the British comprehensive campaign of conquest of the West, the taking of St. Louis by Canadian and Indian allies, could not be prevented, but it did receive a serious setback. De Leyba and the Spaniards were weak, it was true, but they were not entirely surprised by the Canadian attack. De Leyba learned of a British descent of the Mississippi probably by February 1780 and certainly before March 9. They made hasty preparations for the defense of their so-called bastion of the Spanish Illinois country.

De Leyba, without much help from New Orleans, built fortifications which were still incomplete when the British attacked. He called in traders to man the walls, and militiamen arrived from Ste. Geneviève. He dispatched scouts to warn him of the British approach. Alarms of the English and Indian advance were received at Vincennes, Kaskaskia, Cahokia, and St. Louis. Various subordinates of Clark had informed him of an impending attack, many assuming that it would come against Cahokia. In fact, the citizens of Cahokia sent Gratiot to Clark to announce their peril, asking for his help. Gratiot presented Clark with a plan to anticipate the attack on St. Louis and Cahokia—located on opposite sides of the river. He suggested an offensive expedition to scatter the enemy and strike terror among the Indians. The Cahokians were eager to join in such an undertaking. On May 11, 1780, John Montgomery, a captain under George Rogers Clark, left Kaskaskia for Cahokia to prevent the enemy from reaching that village. Montgomery and others also went to de Leyba and suggested a joint expedition to meet the approaching British force. De Leyba promised a hundred equipped men. These offensive tactics, however, did not get underway before the British attacked. But these activities did lead to the Rock River (Illinois) campaign that followed shortly thereafter.

The British struck on May 26, 1780. One division of Indians under Ducharme attacked Cahokia, and the other, including Sac and Fox Indians under one Calvé (a British trader), attacked St. Louis. St. Louis held, partly because of the timely approach of George Rogers Clark with reinforcements. Once under way, the flight of the attackers was headlong. Calvé, Wabasha and the Sioux, and most of the traders retreated up the Mississippi to Prairie du Chien. Others fled up the Illinois River. Clark was obliged to hasten away to meet the threat of Bird's expedition, but before he left he ordered Montgomery to organize a pursuing expedition of three hundred and fifty men, to which de Leyba contributed one hundred. The force marched against Rock River and Prairie du Chien, burning a Sac and Fox village. The supplies at Prairie du Chien, however, were withdrawn by the British before the arrival of the raiders.

The defeat of the British was of far more than local consequence. The failure doomed their ambitious plan to hem in the rebellious American colonies on the west, and the western frontiers of the struggling colonies were in some measure protected from assault. Moreover, Montgomery's expedition against the Sac and Fox demoralized these British allies. They became divided in their allegiance and were buffeted by both sides. Despite their preponderantly British leaning (maintained by British pressure), more of them came over to the Spanish side, at least until the full economic effect of the war was felt. Then lack of aid and supplies may have caused them to waver in their allegiance to the Spaniards.

The defeat of the British-Indian force did not allay the fears of the inhabitants of Spanish Illinois. The inhabitants of St. Louis believed that the British still intended to overrun Illinois and eventually attack Mexico. They implored the governor at New Orleans to send more aid and supplies for their defense. They knew of the activities of British traders among the Indians, and recognized their own inability to compete with British supplies and presents, which apparently prompted Indian raids against scattered farmers and traders. The insecurity of the inhabitants almost led to an abandonment of the Illinois settlements. Yet the Sac Indians proved more faithful to the Spaniards than to the British. Immediately after the Rock River campaign, the majority of the Sac and Fox proved to be of great help to the Spaniards in countering British activities.

De Leyba had been critically ill during the attack of 1780 and died shortly thereafter. Gálvez appointed Francisco Cruzat lieutenant-governor on July 25. Cruzat took over his duties from ad-interim Commandant Silvio Francisco Cartabona de Oro on September 24. Gálvez instructed Cruzat to defend the province against raids by the enemy (British and Indian), to woo Indians from the British to the Spanish side, and to maintain close relationships with American commandants across the river. Cruzat immediately set to his tasks. He stationed Indians and agents along the Mississippi and Illinois rivers to observe British activities and provide timely warnings to St. Louis. Étienne Boucher de Monbreun, with forty Spanish militiamen was stationed at Sac Village just above the mouth of the Des Moines River near modern Montrose, Iowa. Jean Baptiste Malliet, with twelve Spaniards, was stationed on the Illinois River near Peoria. Pierre Dorion, a trader, was sent among the Sioux in 1781. Cruzat was thus able to counteract some British activity among the Sac, Fox, Iowa, Oto, and Pottawatami. Pierre Antaya, a French Canadian from Prairie du Chien, gave Cruzat information about preparations of the British at Green Bay and Prairie du Chien for hostilities against St. Louis to take place during the following spring. As a result, Cruzat paid increasing attention to the defenses of St. Louis, constructing, among other things, a wooden stockade.

Somewhat alarmed by extensive British activity, Cruzat, after carefully weighing alternatives, decided to take the offensive. Canadian merchants were fraternizing and trading with the Indians, persuading some to join the British for the projected attack on Spanish Illinois early in 1781. The Spanish lieutenant-governor knew of the presence of pro-British traders in St. Joseph where supplies were being stockpiled. He learned of De Quindre's defeat of an American party. He became receptive to the pleas of Milwaukee chiefs, El Heturno and Naquiguén, to send a detachment against St. Joseph (with which they would join) in order to check the activities of the traders and their growing influence with the Indians of those regions. All of these facts, Cruzat said, "caused me to send with the above mentioned chiefs, Captain of the militia, Don Eugenio Pouré with a detachment of Spanish and Indians, not withstanding the rigorous winter, to attack St. Joseph." In destroying the supplies and stores at St. Joseph, Cruzat hoped to prevent, or at least make more difficult, a British attack on St. Louis the following spring. It was a shrewd move, reflecting the old military strategy of taking the offensive as a defensive measure.

Leaving St. Louis on January 2, 1781, with a detachment of sixty-five soldiers and sixty Indians, Pouré led his expedition up the Mississippi and Illinois rivers, where the Spanish detachment under Malliet joined the expedition. Ice in the river forced Pouré to abandon his boats and march overland. Surprising Fort St. Joseph, he formally took possession on February 12, and for twenty-four hours the Spanish flag flew over that British outpost. After distributing the captured spoils among the Indians, the expedition returned to St. Louis, reaching the city on March 6.

The St. Joseph expedition was a local, albeit spectacular, and successful military operation in the Upper Mississippi Valley, even though British reports depicted it as a matter of small consequence, an isolated outrage committed by a band of marauders. It did much to bolster Spanish morale and to lower British prestige among the Indians, the objectives included in Cruzat's instructions. The expedition stopped, or at least deterred, enemy attacks—Indian as well as British—thus fulfilling part of Spain's Indian policy of creating alliances for further defense. These methods had been used by Spain before, in Texas and Lower Louisiana against the Apache and English. Later they were to be used in the Southwest. Cruzat hoped that the attack on St. Joseph would engender hostilities between the Milwaukee and pro-British Indians, thereby forcing the former to be loyal to Spain. The safety of the valley demanded compliance with Indian requests. In part, then, Cruzat yielded to the urgings of the Indian chiefs Heturno and Naquiguén because he dared not refuse. Spanish prestige was increased as a result.

Throughout the remainder of the war, the British attempted no other organized official expedition against Spanish Illinois. They did seek to incite the Indians against the Spaniards and to arrange commercial matters, but they were generally unsuccessful. Yet the Mississippi Valley continued to have its share of problems. A rebellion of the settlers, Loyalists and Indians, occurred at Natchez. James Colbert, a pro-British settler, and his Indians raided Spanish settlements and stopped navigation on the river by capturing boats ascending from New Orleans, thus hurting the economy of the upper valley. Spain did take some measures to suppress piracy on the Mississippi, sending troops to Natchez and an expedition to Barrancas de Margot near modern Memphis. The Spanish captain Jacobo Dubreuil also sent an expedition, mainly of Indians, into Chickasaw territory. The Chickasaw asked Cruzat to persuade the North Indians not to attack, and Cruzat laid down conditions for doing such which the Chickasaw accepted. Subsequently, however, Colbert and the Chickasaw attacked the Arkansas Post and laid siege, but Dubreuil successfully withstood that siege. Throughout the war, Cruzat had to pacify pro-Spanish Indians and win pro-British Indians.

The St. Joseph expedition was approved after the fact by the governor at New Orleans and by the Spanish Court. Based on information sent to him by Cruzat, Governor Esteban Rodríguez Miró wrote José de Gálvez, Minister of Charles III, on November 20, 1782, stating that the Americans had abandoned the eastern posts of Illinois. This seemed to him a good time for Gálvez to suggest to His Majesty that the cession of those posts to Spain be obtained from the American Congress. Miró emphasized "the utility and convenience that would result to the state and province" from such action. Gálvez, however, took no action on the matter. Actually the territory had not been abandoned. Troops had been withdrawn from Vincennes and other posts, and civil government had taken the place of military. In reality, too, the preliminary articles of peace between the British and Americans had by then already been drawn up.

Cruzat's chief handicap in governing was still the lack of soldiers and supplies. He bitterly complained of the shortage of presents, so necessary to retain their friendship, for the Indians. He got few presents from headquarters, some of which never reached St. Louis because of pirates and enemies operating on and near the river. Even this meager aid from headquarters was always accompanied by the constant cry to economize "los inmensos dispendios que sufre el Real Erario" (the excessive expenditures which the Royal Exchequer bears). But only gifts could keep the Indians in line. Cruzat's resourcefulness was constantly put to the test. He obtained supplies from the merchants of St. Louis, some of which had been brought up from New Orleans. In this writer's opinion, he also obtained merchandise from British merchants, usually via local traders and merchants who had connections.

Both Cruzat and the British continued their efforts to win over Indians. Cruzat was tireless in this regard. To win the allegiance of those Indians under English jurisdiction as well as those uncommitted, he dispatched men to go among them to change their affections. This was usually the case where British agents were active. For example, Malliet's information of British activities in the upper Great Lakes region, the later Old Northwest, and among the Sioux, had been one cause for Cruzat's expedition against St. Joseph. To combat "evil" influence among the Sioux,

Cruzat sent out trader Pierre Dorion who succeeded in winning them over, except for Chief Oja's important bands. Cruzat also had to keep track of British traders who infiltrated Indian tribes even in Spanish territory; over one hundred traders with canoes, he learned, had been licensed by the British to trade in the Mississippi River region in 1780-81. And in 1782 the British granted licenses to trade in the northwest to owners of one hundred and twenty canoes and two hundred and fifty bateaux with goods valued at £184,000, much of which undoubtedly reached Spanish territory. The British matched the Spaniards in methods aimed at influencing the Indians and succeeded in some instances in winning over bands from Indian families, such as the Sioux, Ottawa, Sac, and Fox, that had previously been, for a time at least, under Spanish influence.

The British were even more successful in infiltrating Spanish-claimed jurisdiction to the north of St. Louis. Traders from Michilimackinac and Prairie du Chien were pouring across the Mississippi River. Without merchandise and supplies, Cruzat and traders got nowhere with the Indians. Even Indians who were, or became, attached to the Spanish begged Cruzat for permission to trade with the British, and Cruzat reluctantly consented. In 1781, a year in which very few or no Spanish traders went out, Joseph Baptiste Parent, who had been trading near Prairie du Chien for a long time with a license from de Leyba, accompanied a number of Indian chiefs to St. Louis to solicit permission to trade with British traders. In a sense this represented the beginning of an end to effective Spanish control of the Upper Mississippi-Missouri region. In 1782, Cruzat informed his superiors that there were more British merchants, with more supplies, than ever before, even in the Mississippi region. Although Cruzat carefully watched the movements and actions of the British, in his efforts to economize, he refused to release from service the detachments which he had sent earlier to the Illinois and Mississippi under Monbreun and Malliet, and which could have been used to hinder British activity.

The peace negotiations affected the Upper Mississippi Valley but little. The territory across the Mississippi formerly belonging to the British was ceded formally to the newly formed United States, at least down to the thirty-first parallel. Spain, regaining the Floridas, became once again master of both sides of the Lower Mississippi and the entire Gulf Coast.

Economically, the war had a tremendous effect, especially upon the upper valley. During the war Spain had been unable to devote much attention to the Spanish Illinois country and few supplies were sent. As a result, the end of the war found the British in complete control of the trade and commerce of the upper parts of the Mississippi Valley. They held a monopoly on Indian trade north of St. Louis and as far west as Missouri. Few Indians remained true to the Spanish cause. The few that did, especially those that had taken part in the St. Joseph campaign, urged Spain to take the offensive against the British at El Estrecho (Detroit). As we have seen, under Cruzat a feeble attempt at resistance was made but the lack of troops, merchandise, and supplies had doomed it to failure from the start.

II

With the English removed, theoretically at least, from the Lower Mississippi Valley and the Gulf Coast, the principal threat to Spanish territory was the westward expansion of the United States. The Indian tribes east of the Mississippi (old Southwest) were of greatest importance to Spain because they could be a barrier against the advancing American frontier. Esteban Miró, who administered Louisiana and West Florida, first as acting governor and then as governor, achieved significant success in dealing with the Indians of the borderland region between the Spanish posts and American settlements.

After 1783, the realignment of the frontiers of Spanish Louisiana created two frontiers along the Mississippi River. One, that below the Ohio River, theoretically south to the thirty-first parallel, and extending to the Atlantic Ocean, was a Spanish-American frontier. Officials along the Spanish-American frontier concerned themselves with the problems of the settling definite boundaries between the United States and Spain, the actual possession of territory between the thirty-first parallel and the Ohio River, the navigation of the Mississippi, and the threats of foreign nations seeking to keep the newly created United States a weak nation, confined on its west by the Appalachian mountains. All of these problems indicated Spain's fear of the aggressive Anglo-Americans, and her desire to use Louisiana as a barrier to, and as protection for, Spain's more valuable possessions in New Spain. These concerns also reflected

Spain's fear of republics in general and propaganda of the French Revolution and intrigues in the West, in particular. After the war, Spain's policy was to establish control over disputed lower Mississippi territory. Miró continued his negotiations with powerful Indians who lived in the disputed area. In this he was aided by the fact that Indians regarded American frontiersmen as their natural enemies.

The disintegration of Spain's colonial empire through Old World wars and New World revolutions broke down Spanish defense and gave the United States an unparalleled opportunity to occupy vast territories in which the beginnings of European civilization had already been introduced. Spain wanted to keep the United States a weak power, in part because it was a republic, and as such philosophically dangerous to her own American colonies. This was one reason why Spain wished to obtain the eastern half of the Mississippi Valley as far north as the Ohio, if not the entire valley. Even after the Treaty of Paris, Spain contrived to ignore the claims of the United States, and held onto the territory north of the thirty-first parallel. Further, she closed the Mississippi to American commerce. By treaties Spain also established protectorates over powerful southern Indian tribes. Many Anglos of West Florida favored the American cause during the war and were not hostile to Spain; some of these crossed into Spanish Louisiana; others went farther west and founded Galveztown, the first Anglo village in Spanish territory.

The Western Americans (Americans living west of the Appalachians) countered Spain's territorial claims by attempting to found colonies in the disputed area. James Robertson initiated a plan to establish a settlement at Chickasaw Bluffs, and land speculator's colonies near Muscle Shoals, Alabama, and in Bourbon County, Georgia.

The Westerners were angry with Spain's closing the Mississippi River. Spain, fearful of direct action by the Westerners and noting rather widespread unrest across the mountains, decided on several plans of action. Spain adopted or tried countercolonization; next, special trade privileges were granted to several favorites; and intrigues were carried on between officials of Spanish Louisiana and the United States West. To parry their fears of George Rogers Clark's rumored recruiting (for France) to pounce upon parts of their empire the Spaniards resorted to intrigue with the greatest of all intriguers, James Wilkinson.

A look at the new Spanish policies, in particular their immigration effort, can be enlightening. Before and during the War, Spain had tried to strengthen Louisiana by encouraging immigration of Spanish, French, German, and other Catholics. Spain invited them and offered many inducements. Few came. Aggressive Anglo-Americans, however, came without invitation or special inducements. Spain was eventually persuaded that an American population in Louisiana would be better than no population, and hoped that the newcomers might become loyal Spanish subjects. That hope was not entirely without basis. Westerners, displeased with the United States government's failure to secure navigation of the Mississippi, talked of separation from the United States and of placing themselves under the protection of Spain.

Spain gave concessions to the American and English settlers. By a royal ordinance dated 1786, all who took an oath of allegiance could remain in Louisiana; passports were issued and liberal land grants given. In 1787 Spain promoted emigration from the United States to Louisiana, opened the Mississippi to commerce, charging a twenty-five per cent duty, and even granted some religious-toleration concessions. There were land promoters and schemers, and some, who, as land speculators, applied to found what perhaps would be semi-independent American colonies. Such, for example, were the applications of Baron Von Steuben, George Rogers Clark, George Morgan, and the Yazoo Land Company. The Spanish government rejected most of these plans. True, George Morgan was permitted to found New Madrid, but his grant was soon revoked. These land speculation schemes did, however, advertise Louisiana. Spanish regulations governing land grants in Louisiana and West Florida were actually more democratic than United States land laws. In general, Spain discouraged land speculation in favor of small-farmer grants which were thought to be the best type. Spanish Louisiana offered reasonable safety, opportunity, freedom from taxation, a market at New Orleans, and kind treatment by local officials.

A change in immigration policy took place under François Hector, Baron de Carondelet, who became governor of Louisiana in 1792. Promotion of American immigration was temporarily abandoned in favor of the establishment of closer alliances with the southern Indians—to protect Spain's northeastern frontier. This was partly due to the protest of the United States against Spain's

colonizing activities in the West, and the fear of invasion of
Louisiana by American frontiersmen in the service of France (i.e.,
as in the case of the Clark-Genêt intrigue).

Although Pinckney's Treaty (Treaty of San Lorenzo, 1795)
reaffirmed Spanish boundaries, it was a diplomatic victory for the
Americans. (It also increased the prospect of war between Spain
and England.) In reality it made already existing frontier conditions
official. Natchez was ceded to the United States, but it was already
largely American. The Mississippi was opened to American
commerce, but some Americans, at least, had been using it for
more than five years. On paper the problems growing out of the
1783 Treaty of Paris peace were settled in favor of the United
States.

Fear that Louisiana might be invaded from Canada when war
threatened between Spain and England in the Nootka Sound
friction led Carondelet to promote once again American
immigration. Beginning in late 1796, a large increase in commerce
on the Mississippi, and other favorable circumstances, stimulated a
rather large American migration into Spanish territory. The
immigrants went largely to Spanish Illinois, West Florida, and in
Lower Louisiana, to the west of the Mississippi, eventually
spreading to Texas. Advertisements for settlers appeared in the
western United States, circulated mainly by Spain's district
commandants. The new immigrants developed agriculture and
industry, especially in Spanish Illinois. West Florida was also
Americanized, in fact faster than the middle valley. Here the fear of
Spanish authorities that an oath of allegiance to His Catholic
Majesty would not make a loyal Spanish subject of Americans was
first confirmed. When Spain delayed the execution of the terms of
the 1795 Treaty of San Lorenzo el Real, the "Spanish subjects" of
Natchez took matters into their own hands and forced the Spanish
governor to recognize the treaty. Spanish troops were finally
withdrawn from north of the thirty-first parallel in 1798, and the
area was organized into Mississippi Territory.

Spain's loss of Natchez resulted in another change in Louisiana's
immigration policy. Spanish officials realized that Anglo-American
settlers might well develop into a menace to the province. Under
Manuel Gayoso de Lemos the entrance of Protestants into Spanish
Louisiana was checked, and Juan Ventura Morales, the intendant,
opposed allowing American immigration into the vicinity adjacent

to Texas since he regarded Americans as a threat to the safety of New Spain. The Anglo-Americans who migrated to Louisiana were not readily assimilated. The original frontier was French and Spanish, with Catholic colonists on either side. But the proportion of Anglo-American immigrants steadily increased, with heavy American population at Rapides and in Ouachita. The Bastrop and Maison Rouge immigration projects brought to Ouachita more colonists from the United States than from Europe. Bayou Bartolomé was cleared and land cultivated, and the land owners began to run cattle. Eventually, the grant to Bastrop was suspended because he was bringing in too many Protestants from the United States. Spanish restrictions were increased: the authority to grant land was placed entirely in the hands of Morales who, in 1799, issued new regulations prejudicial to American immigrants. In 1802, the King forbade the granting of land to United States citizens. But these measures were taken too late to be effective—Americans still entered Louisiana and even Texas. The Spanish policy regarding Texas had always been one of exclusion of foreigners, but before 1800 many Americans had established themselves west of the Sabine.

In the Spanish Illinois country, Upper Louisiana, the story was somewhat different. Here the frontier was officially a Spanish-American one, but in reality it was an Anglo-Spanish borderland. Complicating frontier problems were the contests between British and Americans, Americans and Spaniards, and British and Spaniards. In that triangle of frontier struggles, the Americans played a lesser role until the end of the century. It was British influence that was to dominate the frontier after the Revolutionary War.

As demonstrated earlier, the end of the war found the British in quite complete monopoly of Indian trade on both sides of the Mississippi north of St. Louis. Dated 1784, a memoir on the fur trade, written by the Marquis de Barbé-Marbois, stated that the Spanish, previously of grave concern to the British, were now on the defensive as a result of traders operating out of Canada. Michilimackinac increased in importance as a trade center after the war; traders from Prairie du Chien descended the Mississippi to Spanish Louisiana in spite of the wrath of the Spanish commandants. In 1783, Nicholas Marchesseau, a British-Canadian merchant, opened a trading house in Cahokia and sold merchandise to the Spanish merchants. Goods flowed out of Michilimackinac, through Chicago to the mouth of the Illinois River, and were sold to Spanish traders who paid in peltries. Spanish merchants got supplies from Michilimackinac merchants. These latter also engaged in profitable dealings with the Indians of Upper Louisiana along the Des Moines and St. Peter's rivers. They entered the virgin fur areas in territory which legally belonged to the King of Spain, even though by law they were prohibited from entering territory under his jurisdiction.

The traders at St. Louis could not compete with the British who had better merchandise, were better organized, possessed larger capital, and contended with fewer paternalistic regulations and lower taxes than the Spaniards. Indeed the St. Louis merchants soon found it more advantageous to buy goods shipped down from Montreal than to go to New Orleans. British buyers paid higher prices and had better markets for peltries. By 1783, Auguste Chouteau, Sr., and other Spanish merchants were purchasing merchandise from Marchesseau's store in Cahokia for their Missouri trade. Some of the St. Louis merchants began conducting expeditions to Canada on their own initiative.

Cruzat, meanwhile, had been ordered to keep a watchful eye on the activities of the United States, and he did. He strived to win the friendship of the Indians. He also watched and reported on English activities, such as trade with the Indians, the fortification of Michilimackinac, and the reinforcement of Detroit. In fact, some Indians living east of the Mississippi (among others the Abenaki and the Milwaukee chief El Heturno) even asked Cruzat for permission to move to Spanish territory.

Probably the most convenient summary is to be found in Martín Navarro's 1786 report to the Minister of the Indies, which revealed that the commerce with the Illinois was of little importance because the English from Michilimackinac had swarmed into Spanish territory and seized the richest portion of the trade. "We are compelled to be mere lookers-on, when others do what we ought to do ourselves," said Navarro, "and we have to undergo the vexation of seeing the trade which ought to come down the Mississippi, elude our grasp and take the St. Lawrence for its channel." The English had effectively cornered all the trade with the Indian nations of the Des Moines River, only eighty leagues above St. Louis.

Cruzat's attention, however, was largely occupied with the problem of subjugating the Osage. Although fairly peaceable in the Spanish Illinois region—they received their annuities from St. Louis—they harassed traders and other Indians along the upper Arkansas and terrified both reds and whites in the neighborhood of the Natchitoches post and Texas border. To accomplish the almost impossible task of subduing and controlling the Osage, the Spaniards used various methods: stopping or withholding annuities; prohibiting trade with them; and ultimately, utilizing punitive measures, including war. When overawed, the Osage would generally sue for peace; but almost as soon as it was granted, and it often was, they would resume their depredations on Spanish settlements. While Cruzat was lieutenant-governor in St. Louis, a conference was proposed (which was to be held on a boat in the Natchitoches River) to determine the means to be taken to exterminate the hated Osage. The problem was compounded by the question of who held jurisdiction over the Osage. Officially they were under the jurisdiction of St. Louis, but the Arkansas posts had traders who would intrigue and carry on trade with them even when St. Louis prohibited it. Similar actions took place in other localities. At one time the Osage, Caddodacho, and other Indians went to New Orleans and a peace was made there, but that peace could not be maintained because of what the Spaniards termed "the perfidious conduct of the Osage Indians." Osage-Caddodacho warfare intensified the jurisdictional quarrels between the commandant of Arkansas and the lieutenant-governor at St. Louis. The Arkansas Indians wanted to combine forces with other Indians to war on the Osage. At least three or four times preparations were begun to wage war on the Osage, but outside factors prevented the Spaniards from carrying out such full-scale measures against them. The Osage were reported to have between eight and nine hundred warriors. Using Indians to make war on them would be very expensive and not effective. Fear that the Osage would get their supplies from the English was a potent factor in stopping war. Jealousy of traders and clashes of economic interests between the hunters and traders of the various local posts also prevented all-out war.

On November 27, 1787, Cruzat was succeeded as lieutenant-governor in St. Louis by Manuel Pérez. Pérez was an experienced soldier. His administration, however, was marked by the advance of British influence over the Indians and the reduction of Spanish influence in the Upper Mississippi. Still, being a good bureaucrat, Pérez kept his ears to the ground and reported fully any and all rumors of British activity among the Indians. He reported on November 9, 1788, that the British were sending goods via the Indians of the Mississippi to the Missouri, "where they [English] go to trade" and that even the Osage were being supplied by the British.

Pérez was faced with two serious problems: stopping the increasing incursions by British and Americans into territory under Spanish jurisdiction; and improving the defenses of Spanish Illinois. During these troublesome years, when the Osage were most hostile to the Spaniards, the Spanish government wished to deprive them of all provisions in order to reduce them to obedience. The Osage, however, were able to go to the Des Moines River and get provisions from British traders. The war planned against the Osage had to be called off because of fear of the Clark-Genêt intrigues and the projected British attack of Spanish Louisiana. Carondelet knew, however, that the Osage had to be pacified. Therefore, in 1794, he granted the exclusive trading rights with them to Auguste Chouteau, Sr., who promised to build and maintain a fort among the Osage.

During Pérez' regime two large incursions were made into the Spanish Illinois country. One was American at L'Anse à la Graisse, which resulted in the establishment of New Madrid in 1789. The other was a British expedition from the north. There were others by Americans, British, and Canadians in the regions of the White, Ouachita, and other rivers south of St. Louis.

In the face of these incursions, and fearful of a British or American attack upon the Spanish Illinois, Pérez, as early as 1788, observed the worthlessness of the fortifications of St. Louis, and urged construction of stone bastions to replace the old wooden ones built by Cruzat in 1781. He also advised filling gaps in the militias, especially the one at St. Louis, which had been on part strength for a long time.

Under Pérez the Spanish policy of Indian countercolonization had success. He encouraged friendly tribes to cross the Mississippi and settle in Spanish Illinois. Louis Lorimier, friendly to the Spaniards, led some Shawnee across the river and settled near Cape Girardeau. Lorimier enticed other tribesmen to follow the example of the Shawnee.

The closing years of Pérez' regime marked a decline in Spanish control of the territory. The British had organized their aggressive Northwest Company, which traded legally in American territory, illegally in Spanish territory, and controlled and influenced the Indians in both areas. From Michilimackinac, the British led trade expeditions along the Mississippi, Iowa, and Minnesota rivers. They not only traded with the Indians but with the Spaniards from St. Louis and Ste. Geneviève. The Spaniards did retain control of the Mississippi River trade, at least to the south. To prevent incursions they tried to incite Sac Indians against American traders.

From experience, Pérez advised and suggested to his superiors that the only way to stop the British incursions into the trans-Mississippi west was to construct forts and establish garrisons at the mouth of the Des Moines River, the entrance to the Iowa and Missouri-Platte area, and at the mouth of the St. Peter's River, the gateway to the rich fur area of the Minnesota country. Pérez warned that the British were not only swarming into that area, but were trading on the Missouri and Platte rivers. He also warned the Spanish higher echelon that the English and the Americans spoke of nothing but the Kingdom of Mexico, and of ways to see and penetrate it. In 1790, the greater part of merchandise for the Missouri trade was brought to Cahokia from Michilimackinac, partly by Spanish subjects themselves, and partly by British traders. William Doyle, commanding the British post at Michilimackinac, wrote in mid-1793, that the most considerable trade from his post was up to and beyond the Mississippi by the route of Prairie du Chien. Most assuredly Pérez, and later Zenon Trudeau, his successor, were not ignorant of this illegal or contraband trade. Both, and Trudeau certainly, winked at that illegal trade which brought prosperity to the province—especially since they could not remedy the situation. Pérez had tried to prevent British infiltration into the Iowa country by befriending the Sac and Fox Indians, but these Indians remained hostile and proved to be his nemesis.

Trouble which would have a decided effect upon the frontiers of the Mississippi Valley, had also been brewing in other parts of the world. In 1790, the Nootka Sound Controversy on the Northwest coast almost brought Spain and England to blows. Pérez at St. Louis counseled that an increase of forces would be necessary, for the Spanish officials feared that the British might attack Louisiana. Spain was equally fearful lest the United States, in retaliation for the closure of the Mississippi to Americans, would allow British soldiers to cross American territory and thus facilitate a British attack from Canada upon Spanish territory in the Mississippi Valley. No real efforts were actually made, however, to reinforce Upper Louisiana for a few years to come.

Meanwhile, the failure of the Spanish government to keep the lower reaches of the river safe for commerce, its obstinacy in maintaining tariffs and other regulations, and the superiority of the British goods and methods, gave the British an advantage which all the diplomatic and military skills of Cruzat and Pérez, and the astuteness of the French traders at St. Louis, could not overcome. St. Louisans were forced during the next decade to turn to the Indian tribes of the Upper Missouri region for trade. Even in this remote region they met with severe competition from the powerful British companies.

Pérez' health broke down and he resigned his lieutenant-governorship at St. Louis. He was succeeded by Zenon Trudeau. Shortly before, Miró's ten-year regime had also come to an end, and he was succeeded by the Baron de Carondelet as governor-general of Louisiana. With the coming of Carondelet and Trudeau, renewed life and vigor characterized local Spanish officialdom. Both men were more practical and vigorous than their predecessors in resisting British encroachment, and in disciplining unruly Indian tribes. Belated steps to stem the tide of the British and American invasions were taken. The frontiers of Spanish Louisiana divided and shifted. In order to understand this process, we must deal first with Spanish activities before Lewis and Clark and Pike took over the Spanish frontier and put an end to the ideas and problems, ideals and desires, which characterized the twilight years of Spanish rule in the Upper Mississippi-Missouri valleys.

III

In Lower Mississippi, the Baron de Carondelet was confronted with serious and diverse problems of frontier defense. We omit here his problems with the adventurer William Augustus Bowles along the Florida-Georgia frontier. American activities among the Indians of the south countered Spain's previous successes with them. The Westerners were still threatening to open the Mississippi River by force. The government of the United States was getting stronger and was still demanding free navigation of the Mississippi and observance of the thirty-first parallel boundary. West of the Mississippi, the Osage continued to terrorize the settlements; Louisiana traders sold arms which reached Lipan Apache; and Choctaw and Chickasaw Indians increased their raiding. To these ever present problems was now added the major problem caused by the French Revolution and war between Spain and France. Jacobin agitation among the French inhabitants of the Mississippi Valley, and the organization of filibustering expeditions in the American West under French auspices, seriously threatened the safety of Louisiana.

Guarding such a long front with very few troops, utilizing militias in which he had little or no confidence, and relying on friendly Indians who were less than trustworthy, at best, hampered Carondelet. His pleas for men, money, supplies, and naval help mostly went unheeded. His only advantage was that he had a few able, experienced subordinate officials, such as Zenon Trudeau at St. Louis and Gayoso de Lemos at Natchez.

So serious was the situation that Carondelet wrote to John Graves Simcoe, lieutenant-governor of Upper Canada, soliciting an English alliance against the Americans in the West. Simcoe was sympathetic, but could give no help since he was busy contending with the troops of American general Anthony Wayne in the Old Northwest.

Meanwhile, Spain, that is Minister Godoy, had also had as its first aim checking the American frontiersmen's progress through Spain's frontiers. Since that had appeared impossible, Godoy preferred a treaty with the established government of the United States to an intrigue with its irresponsible frontiersmen. War, real and rumored, was in the air when the Treaty of San Lorenzo (1795) was ordered enforced. In fact that treaty had been made just in case war broke out between England and Spain as a result of Godoy's European diplomacy. The Spanish Court had sent orders to oust the British and drive out the unlicensed traders from the Missouri valley. Indeed, that was to be one of the reasons for declaring war on England in 1796. Carondelet realized, and sought to avert, the threat to Spain's tenuous hold upon Louisiana that was manifested in the vast western surge of American emigration, and the persistent penetration of British traders into the upper reaches of the Mississippi Valley.

Godoy, who had signed the Treaty of San Lorenzo el Real in 1795, issued orders to evacuate the territory ceded by that treaty to the United States. This Carondelet reluctantly proceeded to do. However, when Carondelet learned of the declaration of war between Spain and England and the work of Collot, Lieutenant-colonel Carlos Howard, and Thomas Power (not to mention Blount's conspiracy), he countermanded the order to evacuate the territory ceded and prepared for the defense of Spain's possessions in the Mississippi Valley. Carondelet's orders were given too late to prevent John Pope and Andrew Ellicott from occupying Natchez. Hence Nogales became the focal point of any defense. Forced to take a stand on his own initiative, Carondelet gave alternative instructions to his Nogales commandant. He was to evacuate if necessary, on the basis of the treaty, provided he could get the Americans to guarantee support in case of an English attack against Louisiana. If there should be the slightest chance for success, however, he was to stand and fight. These instructions were quite naturally secret. To cover up and keep the inhabitants of the area quiet, Carondelet published two proclamations, dated May 24 and 31, stating that due to possible attacks upon Louisiana by the British from Canada and by the Americans he was delaying the evacuation of the posts. These proclamations failed to quiet the inhabitants. In fine: The crisis of 1797 centered upon the retention of Fort Nogales which was regarded by Spain as essential for the defense of Louisiana and the control of the Choctaw Indians. Neither Carondelet nor his successor, Gayoso de Lemos, yielded. After the death of the latter, Nogales was given up only on direct orders from the King.

With Fort San Fernando evacuated, and Nogales and Natchez relinquished to the Americans, defenses naturally shifted to New Orleans and to Placaminas, sixty miles south. The shift from the principal defense in the north or upper river to the south or lower river was made imperative by local conditions. St. Louis, despite Collot's argument that it was an essential point for the defense, could not in reality be fortified properly nor given troops and other materials sufficient to stop any invading regular armies; adequate defense would be neither possible nor financially feasible, since in addition it would have required maintaining a fleet in the upper river. Furthermore, St. Louis was too far north to serve as a year-round naval base for vessels as large as galleys. It was decided that St. Louis was to be fortified only against Indian raids, or attacks not supported by artillery. It was known that the fall of St. Louis would presage the loss of Lower Louisiana, the loss of the Missouri Valley, and the consolidation of English power on the Pacific coast. Thus, Anglo-Spanish rivalry continued, and Spain sent its gunboats to patrol the upper Mississippi nearly every year until the change of ownership took place in 1805.

Yielding to an appeal from the Spanish representative in the United States, President Washington issued a proclamation March 24, 1794, designed to break up unauthorized military demonstrations in the West, specifically on the Ohio. This removed one threat to Spain in the Mississippi, but added another. General Anthony Wayne sent a Captain Doyle to construct a fort on the lower Ohio to prevent any American military movement downriver against Louisiana. But Spain regarded this fort (Fort Massac) as a threat equal to G.R. Clark's invasion. Carondelet ordered troops sent to Thomas Portell, commandant at New Madrid, and bade him watch American activities closely. Carondelet saw in American Fort Massac on the Ohio a confirmation of his suspicions concerning the expansionist designs of the Americans. On May 19, 1794, Carondelet warned his home government that the Americans were more to be feared in the Mississippi Valley than the French and predicted that they would ultimately absorb Louisiana.

Throughout 1794, Spain was compelled to watch the fate of her Mississippi Valley possessions being determined by events on the American frontier. Wayne's American victory at Fallen Timbers broke the power of the Indians north of the Ohio, and General James Robertson's attack on Creek and Cherokee subdued those powerful tribes. The southern tribes were intent on making peace with the Americans. Thus Carondelet's plan for using Indians as defense against the United States was rendered ineffective. His desire to take advantage of separatist movements in the American West was also frustrated, for the government of Spain decided to abandon any such plan and, instead, attempt to conciliate the United States. Further, the crushing of the Whiskey Rebellion quelled the separatist tendencies of the American Westerners.

On November 24, 1794, Carondelet wrote a detailed military report in which he analyzed the dangers of American expansion.

He warned his government that, unless Spain sent heavy troop reinforcements to Louisiana and employed every possible means of defense, the Americans would not be stopped at the Mississippi. Carondelet believed that a general revolution threatened Spain in America unless a powerful and speedy remedy was applied.

In his determination to protect the province which he predicted in a few years could become equal, or perhaps surpass the American western states in fertility, cultivation, trade and wealth, Carondelet laid broad plans for checking the American advance. There was to be a line of forts along the Mississippi, militia to be organized, ready to rush to any threatened point, and galleys and swift gunboats to patrol the river. Indian allies, fifteen hundred strong, were to form a second line of defense. St. Louis at the northern end of the military zone was to guard Spanish settlements from the mouth of the Missouri to New Madrid.

Carondelet selected and appointed a special military commandant for the Upper Louisiana country, an Irishman, Lieutenant-colonel Carlos Howard. He was to dismantle Fort San Fernando, built by Gayoso de Lemos to extend and protect Spain's military frontier. (It was also used to check the activities of American land companies.) Howard was then to fortify St. Louis and prepare its defense against an expected British attack from Canada, drive the British out of the Upper Missouri and Upper Mississippi, and stamp out sedition which it was feared had been increasing in the upper part of Spanish Louisiana.

Howard, together with the squadron of river war vessels, ascended the Mississippi and performed his tasks. He secretly dismantled and evacuated Fort San Fernando de las Barrancas. He went north to strengthen the defenses of New Madrid, and took charge in St. Louis. Galliots were sent to cruise at or near the mouth of the Des Moines River, with orders to arrest all unlicensed traders found operating in Spanish territory. He suppressed British trade, attempted to foment rebellion in Canada, sent spies to Prairie du Chien, Chicago, and Philadelphia, and established an outpost at the mouth of the Illinois River. Howard then returned downriver. By then the scene had shifted once again from the Upper to Lower Mississippi, and with it the focus of defense of the frontiers of Spanish Louisiana.

The 1795 Treaty had constituted a death blow to the defense of Louisiana. Gayoso de Lemos warned that the "moment His

Majesty loses dominion over the Mississippi an equal fate will be decreed for the Kingdom of Mexico." Despite all, Spain followed previous policy: promoting immigration, especially of European Catholics, into Lower Louisiana, continuing the Kentucky intrigue in the face of hostility of Westerners and mutual jealousy of the conspirators, and courting and trying to keep the friendship of the southern Indians. In addition, there was a deterioration in the character of the higher officials of Louisiana, and infighting between the intendant and governor-general. Adventurers entered the province, of whom Philip Nolan and William Bowles are only the best known. And expenditures exceeded revenue, making Louisiana very costly. The value of Louisiana as a barrier to the Provincias Internas of Mexico came into question. Gayoso warned that the surrender of territory and the granting of free navigation of the Mississippi under the Treaty of 1795, endangered both Louisiana and New Spain, and would lead to contraband trade with the Provincias Internas. He acknowledged that it would be very costly to make Louisiana a barrier, but maintained that it was necessary to prevent the loss of Mexico. He suggested that Baton Rouge be made an important military post, and fortified and garrisoned heavily; that a line of blockhouses be established along the river, especially the lower river; and that settlements be formed opposite Natchez. He saw as necessities military posts along the Mississippi, completion of the defense of St. Louis, and naval squadrons to patrol the river. He urged that free trade be established at New Orleans, a full regiment be added to the military forces there and a new battalion sent to Pensacola. Finally, Gayoso urged Francisco de Saavedra, who had succeeded Godoy as Minister in Spain in 1798, to draw the boundary line in the north from the Lake of the Woods to the Pacific, keeping the Colorado River well within the boundaries of Spain. Furthermore, Gayoso recommended fortifying Arkansas Post, increasing the number of galleys patroling the mouth of the Mississippi, and keeping militias in readiness, and supplied. All of that would be costly indeed. Therefore, the Spanish policy after San Lorenzo was to try to separate the United States West from the central government. (Spain also hoped and expected a rupture between the United States and France, and planned to side with France.)

The Treaty of San Lorenzo caused the first and widest breach in the so-called protective wall, Louisiana. The Americans lost no time in taking full advantage of their gains by this treaty. They swarmed down the Mississippi River eager to develop their newly acquired trade route. American settlers, encouraged by Spanish authorities, moved into Louisiana in large numbers. The American central government was now functioning with vigor and unity, and Spanish authorities had demonstrated their weakness. By the end of the century Louisiana had become much less valuable; it was, in fact, a useless, and costly, barrier in the possession of Spain. It most obviously was not checking the Americans.

The forced, secret retrocession of Louisiana to France in 1800 caused the United States and especially the Westerners considerable alarm. This was compounded when Intendant Juan Ventura Morales closed the right of deposit at New Orleans to the Americans. The Westerners threatened and fumed; the government of Thomas Jefferson went to work and in the end purchased the whole of what was by then, at least in name, once again French Louisiana.

The barrier thus succumbed to the relentless pressure of Western American frontiersmen and settlers. By 1795 it consisted only of Louisiana west of the Mississippi River, the area south to the thirty-first parallel, and West and East Florida. This new barrier was to prove too fragile to withstand the lashing of the westward tide, and it fell in sections, until it no longer existed.

3

Before Zebulon Montgomery Pike: The Frontier on the Upper Mississippi during the later years of Spanish Rule

Zebulon Montgomery Pike, the first American official to be sent up the Mississippi after the United States acquired both sides of the river by virtue of the Louisiana Purchase, found British fur traders occupying both banks as well as the surrounding back country, and the British generally in control of the Indians. Pike, of course, announced formally that the entire area now belonged to the United States, warning all foreigners to leave and requesting all Indians to acknowledge the Great White Father in distant Washington. As we know, he was successful, for British traders retained their virtual monopoly of the area of the Upper Mississippi until another "war for independence" was fought with England—the War of 1812.

Official boundary lines as they existed in formal treaties had no bearing on the actual situation. True, international "law" should have taken effect, but such ideals—and they were generally no more than that—never entered the minds of aggressive frontiersmen and Indian traders. They were there, and they acted with the usually effective bargaining agents—bad whiskey, furs, presents, goods in quantity, and plenty of advice—despite protests and international diplomacy in capitals far from the actual scene. What Pike saw, and what the actual conditions constituted, was the Anglo-Spanish frontier story.

The critical situation in which Spain found herself in the Mississippi Valley after withdrawing from her alliance with England (by signing the Treaty of Basle) and in trying to improve her situation with the United States in 1795 (by signing the Treaty of San Lorenzo el Real, or Pinckney's Treaty) forced her to take steps toward the defense of her provinces. War broke out in

October 1796, shortly after the ratification of Pinckney's Treaty, complicating the situation for Spain, and posing a threat to her territory from British Canada and possibly, too, from the United States.

The Spanish government had acceded to the American demands in Pinckney's Treaty, a thing which local Spanish officials disliked. Baron de Carondelet, governor-general of Louisiana, was ordered to carry out the Treaty's provisions. Carondelet had problems. He knew of the difficult situation stemming from Spanish intrigues with the Indians and Westerners. Also, English and Canadian traders were swarming into Spanish territory in the Upper Mississippi Valley. And, as usual, there were the threats and cajolings of the French with which to contend.

The Mississippi River officially became the boundary between Spain and England in 1763, and for our purposes remained so until 1804. Treaty alterations in 1783, 1794, and 1795 did not change the situation in the Upper Mississippi Valley. What did affect local activities was the fact that Spain owned, but did not effectively control, all of the trans-Mississippi West to the Pacific Ocean; on the other hand, England owned and did effectively control an area reaching across the entire continent, and occupied territory east of the Upper Mississippi. The ineffectively colonized, and in fact unexplored, no-man's-land separating Spain's northeastern frontier from the Interior Provinces, the unknown sources of the Mississippi River, and an undefined frontier led to repeated British aggression and Spanish threats of retaliation. This was interspersed with Spanish attempts during periods of stress and warfare to take aggressive action against the money-making, canny Scotsmen and French-Canadian *coureurs de bois.* The latter were aroused by potential monetary gain, and aided and abetted by plentiful supplies of merchandise, presents, bad whiskey, advice, and some governmental support. Spain, on the other hand, was off base when it came to government action; it lacked money and merchandise, and was hampered by its bureaucracy and uncooperative government officials. The official decision to use the vast Spanish territory of Louisiana almost solely as a barrier to protect the more valuable mineral-laden colonies of New Spain, forced the unhappy residents and traders of the Spanish Illinois country to depend on their own resources, poor as they were, to protect themselves. As a result some Spanish officials followed common sense rather than law for the purpose of self-preservation and the making of a livelihood. Local as well as more distant Spaniards were still Spaniards in character, and as such, were extremely fearful of the more aggressive Anglo-Saxon. They leaned on other devices to hold onto their patrimony.

II

The keys to the Anglo-Spanish frontier along the five-hundred-mile stretch of the winding Mississippi River were St. Louis and Prairie du Chien. The Spaniards tried to make St. Louis a bastion of defense, for if St. Louis should fall, the whole Upper Mississippi would slip into British hands and the frontier line would drop to Nogales or even to New Orleans. From there, attacked from the east and along the south, the Spaniards could be pushed into Texas and beyond. The Interior Provinces of New Spain were also endangered by the aggressive Americans pushing west and by the perceptive British, relentlessly pushing southwest from Canada.

To counter these movements, Spain made a last attempt in the final decades of the eighteenth century to extend its influence northward, as explained in chapter four, which I have called "Before Lewis and Clark." They pushed north from their preciously guarded Santa Fe and reached St. Louis, thus connecting their separated provinces; they also went north up the backbone of the Rocky Mountains to connect with their northeastern boundary. This is what I have called "Genesis of the Santa Fe Trail" (chapter five). In addition, the Spaniards pushed northward up the Pacific coast and westward from Santa Fe to California. In this context, then, the history of the Upper Mississippi is what I call "Before Zebulon Montgomery Pike," since events there were soon followed by Pike's expedition on the Upper Mississippi.

North of the Arkansas River and west of the Mississippi lay the territory known to the Spaniards as Spanish Illinois. The capital of this area was St. Louis, strategically located just south of the mouth of the Missouri on the west bank of the Mississippi. Protected on the east and north by the waters of the two rivers, the capital of Spanish Illinois faced the territory of the British. Here the traders, often French or Canadian by birth and upbringing, but

Spanish in their allegiance, congregated. From St. Louis, subjects of His Catholic Majesty spread up and down nearly every river whose waters emptied into the Mississippi.

Far up the Missouri, the Kansas, the Osage, and the Platte rivers the Spaniards went in quest of furs. Into the waters of the Upper Mississippi, Ohio, Illinois, Wisconsin, and other rivers flowing into the "Father of Waters" from the east went Spanish canoes. From the regions of St. Joseph, Maumee, the Wabash posts, Wisconsin, Michigan, Illinois, and Indiana, the Indians brought their furs to St. Louis.

Five hundred miles above the mouth of the Missouri, at the junction of the Wisconsin and the Mississippi, an equally strategic point, was quaint old Prairie du Chien owned by the British. Guarded on the west by the Mississippi and on the south by the waters of the Wisconsin, Prairie du Chien looked with covetous eye upon the rich fur lands across the Mississippi. It was a convenient meeting place for Indians and traders operating in the Upper Mississippi Valley, and it was a taking-off point for the traders and voyageurs. From Prairie du Chien, British traders swarmed across the Mississippi, ascended the St. Peter's, Des Moines, Iowa, Skunk, and other rivers to tap virgin fur-field riches. They pushed directly across the Iowa country to the Missouri, and southwest toward the Interior Provinces of New Spain. In the far northwest they trapped and traded with the Indians in violation of international and Spanish law, unmolested by Spanish officials and encouraged by the British.

At first, on taking over Louisiana, Spain adopted a vigorous Indian policy that embodied French ideas, and succeeded in winning and maintaining the friendship of numerous Indian tribes. Officials also managed to keep the British and other foreigners out of Spanish territory. They captured a number of intruders and protested British activity to British frontier officials. (So, too, did Spaniards enter their rivals' territory, and many British protests were made to Spanish frontier officials.) In general, the Spaniards were effective in about a one-hundred-and-fifty-mile radius around St. Louis. But in the Iowa-Minnesota area, British traders held free sway. They entered the country without being disturbed and through trade, flattery, and gifts succeeded in winning the allegiance of many tribes. Britishers such as Jonathan Carver and Peter Pond explored and traded, and by 1778 at least a dozen or more firms held British licenses to trade in the Illinois country, on the Mississippi River, and around Prairie du Chien. Sometimes when they were close to St. Louis, the Spaniards would catch and successfully deal with some of them. Such, for example, was the case of Juan María (Jean Marie) Ducharme who, in 1773, while trading with the Little Osage along the Missouri, was forced to flee from Spanish soldiers, leaving his goods behind.

During the American Revolution, Spain gained an early advantage in the Upper Valley, but this advantage was shortlived. Spain entered that war in 1779, and after a few skirmishes or near skirmishes in defense of St. Louis against British attack, temporarily invaded British territory. Time was on the side of the British, however, who had won overwhelming control of the Indians and trade of the Upper Mississippi Valley because of the inability of Spain to supply goods and presents to the Indians. In fact, some Spanish settlements had to resort to drawing supplies and merchandise from British firms. This increased effective British control of the Indians and Indian trade in the entire Upper Mississippi Valley had even allowed British traders to extend operations westward to the Upper Missouri area, a fact known early by the Spaniards. In 1786, Intendant Martín Navarro reported on it, expressing regret that the Spaniards had to be mere onlookers at a trade that rightfully and by nature should be descending the Mississippi to New Orleans, but which instead was being carried on via Michilimackinac. Not only did that English furtrading mecca prosper, but the British also took over the trade of all the Indian nations of the Des Moines River, which was but eighty leagues above St. Louis. In 1784 François de Barbé-Marbois, the French chargé d'affaires in the United States, stated that before the American Revolution the Spaniards had caused British authorities in the Illinois country no little concern, but since that time had been on the defensive.

Spanish officials alerted their government to the British menace, and some Spanish officers suggested means of combating it. The American Governor of the Northwest Territory, Arthur St. Clair, however, reported that, despite some risks, trade possibilities were good in Spanish territory. After 1788, and particularly after 1791, the Spanish lieutenant-governors of St. Louis advised their superiors that the only way to stop British incursions into the trans-Mississippi country was to construct forts at the mouth of the

Des Moines River (the entrance into the Iowa and the Middle Missouri-Platte area), and at the mouth of the St. Peter's River (the gateway to the rich fur area of the Minnesota country). In fact, in 1791 Manual Pérez, then Spanish lieutenant-governor of St. Louis, warned of the British ambition to get to the Kingdom of Mexico. But no real effort on the part of Spain to reinforce Upper Louisiana came until years later.

After 1790 the British openly admitted that most of the posts where their traders wintered were within the limits claimed by Americans, while several of the trading places along the Mississippi were on the Spanish side. British and Spanish sources bear this out.

Zenon Trudeau told Carondelet on November 12, 1792, that the Spaniards were unable to trade with the Indians of the Mississippi, for the river was filled with Englishmen from Michilimackinac; at least one hundred and fifty canoes from there, each loaded with two or three thousand pesos worth of merchandise, had been counted. In 1793 Trudeau again reported on the superiority of English commerce with the Indians, and listed canoes on the St. Peter's, Des Moines, Skunk, Iowa, and other rivers. Robert Dickson, an active British trader on the Upper Mississippi, described the extremely valuable fur trade. Captain Doyle, commandant at Michilimackinac, confirmed Dickson's description. He observed that the most considerable trade from his post was to and beyond the Mississippi by route of Prairie du Chien, from which place the traders also carried on a considerable trade with St. Louis; that some Spanish merchants had come to Michilimackinac to trade; that a chain of British traders extended from Illinois up the Mississippi to the mouth of the St. Peter's River; and that the trade up the big river was the most valuable branch of commerce belonging to the Michilimackinac post. Such reports are to be found for almost every year from then on. Canadian Lieutenant-governor John Graves Simcoe suggested that he would like to see a British factory built on the western bank of the Mississippi, perhaps opposite the mouth of the Wisconsin River; if it could be done without exciting the jealousy of Spain. Charles Stevenson, with the British in Canada, was anxious to negotiate a commercial treaty with Spain, which would grant the British effective navigation of the Mississippi. The quid pro quo could perhaps be a British guarantee of Spain's American possessions.

On April 30, 1795, Trudeau wrote the Baron de Carondelet and enclosed a request from Duchêne Pero—the only trader from his district working along the Des Moines River—suggesting the establishment of posts on the Mississippi to oppose the British traders, and the making of an agreement with the London government regulating trade. Trudeau urged that a small armed galliot patrol the river for three months during each year. He also notified the commandant at Mackinac that he would arrest all British traders found in Spanish territory.

In December 1795, Andrew Todd, a Canadian merchant who transferred his allegiance to Spain, told the Spanish governor-general that it was well-known that, despite the vigilance of the Spanish government, the traders from Michilimackinac were in sole possession of trade in the upper parts of the province, and that they maintained it because they were free from duties on imported and exported goods.

III

By 1792, a change had taken place in the administrative personnel; Zenon Trudeau became lieutenant-governor at St. Louis and the Baron de Carondelet, governor-general at New Orleans. Trudeau was a likeable person, endowed with a lot of common sense. Although loyal and patriotic to Spain, he understood the local situation and acted in accordance with practicalities rather than tie himself to the endless rigor of Spanish law. He ignored the fact, for example, that some British merchants and traders carried on business with the merchants of St. Louis.

Trudeau objected emphatically, however, to British traders entering Spanish territory to trade with the Indians. Should these foreigners capture the trade with the Indian nations in Spanish territory, several detrimental results were likely to follow. In the first place, the profit would be denied Spanish residents. In their rivalry with Spanish traders, the British would imbue the Indians with a hatred for the Spanish; and, giving vent to their aroused feeling against the subjects of Spain, the Indian nations would "pounce" upon the Spaniards, pillage their towns, and tomahawk the settlers. A combination of motives—patriotism, economics, and self-defense—forced Trudeau to attempt to stop the influx of British traders into Spanish territory. The Spanish Court had turned a deaf ear to all of Trudeau's recommendations. Critical times in Spain, remoteness of the Illinois country from New Orleans and of the latter from Spain, and the fear of spending money, which indeed was scarce, were but a few of the reasons why Spain did not, in fact could not, accede to Trudeau and Carondelet's requests. Carondelet did what he could with his very limited supplies of goods and money and the small number of ships and men.

In 1793, Trudeau dispatched an expedition of some forty men under a sergeant to the Des Moines River to arrest all foreign traders in the area. This expedition captured some English traders descending the Mississippi about forty-one leagues above St. Louis, near the confluence of the Mississippi and Des Moines rivers. The goods confiscated belonged to Andrew Todd (of Todd, McGill and Company, merchants of Montreal) and the English-Canadian Traders Josiah Bleakley and Nicholas Marchesseau. The men captured included two of the principals, who were brought to St. Louis. They protested that they had been trading without molestation for years. Todd's capture in particular turned out to be fortunate for the Spanish, as well as profitable for him, as we shall see shortly.

Both Trudeau and Carondelet took advantage of any and all opportunities to cope with the situation. They granted exclusive monopolies to the Missouri Company, a fur trading group formed in 1794, hoping thus to oust the British from the Upper Missouri. But by 1796 it was difficult for the Spaniards even to penetrate to the Upper Missouri. The tribes of the Lower Missouri were being indoctrinated by the British, and the Upper Mississippi was daily becoming infested with British traders and trappers—all coming from Michilimackinac through Prairie de Chien, despite every possible effort on the part of Trudeau and Carondelet.

As a last resort Carondelet conceived the idea of fighting the British with their own fire, taking advantage of the capture of Andrew Todd. Todd, not wishing to lose all, and knowing that to continue his lucrative business in the Upper Mississippi meant working under either American or Spanish jurisdiction, offered to change his allegiance to Spain. This writer believes that Todd had had some previous connections with St. Louis merchants, notably Jacques Clamorgan, and was perhaps a supplier of merchandise to Clamorgan's Missouri Company. The Chouteaus, and others had very certainly been dealing with Todd, McGill and Company, and with William Grant, who visited St. Louis; Gabriel Cerré, Charles Gratiot and others similarly dealt with Canadian merchant houses.

As a starter, Clamorgan petitioned Carondelet, offering to finance and construct a fort at the mouth of the Des Moines River in order to stop British incursions into Spanish territory. In return, he asked for an exclusive trading privilege with the Indians residing near, or frequenting, the Des Moines, Skunk, and Iowa rivers, and their tributaries, for a term of six years. Although Andrew Todd's name is not mentioned in this document, the sequel persuades this writer that Todd was behind it; for Todd got the exclusive trade of the Mississippi above St. Louis, which was respected after Spain granted and confirmed the original petition. Subsequently, Todd proposed many changes in the contract, as well as an extension of the grant from six to ten years. He also asked for troops to guard the proposed forts. The original petition called for compensation for Todd's seized goods, for the privilege of supplying the trade and merchants, and for goods for his Indian trade to be imported into Louisiana at the low duty of six percent instead of the regular fifteen percent to twenty-one percent. Carondelet placed great reliance on what Todd promised to do—namely, drive out the Mackinac traders from the region—and granted the concession without even waiting for approval from the Spanish Court (which came much later).

Things were beginning to look a bit rosier for Carondelet and Trudeau. In fact, there were immediate results. Trudeau, with Carondelet's blessing, even gave modest aid to Todd's *caxeros* on the Mississippi—especially those sent to the Des Moines River, where they met the British who, to the practical exclusion of Spaniards, had infested the area. This aid consisted of a corporal and two soldiers. They were to remain two months for the purpose of ordering any Englishmen or Americans to retire, and, if they refused, to capture them and their boats and goods. All of this was to be done, of course, without incurring any expenses to the royal treasury; Todd supplied the troops with all necessary provisions. This step, as one might guess, proved ineffective, for the corporal and two soldiers were not sufficient strength, and the British and Americans simply laughed at them. In fact, several of Todd's traders were forced to retreat in the face of British-induced Indian hostilities.

Todd's men requested forces from Trudeau to protect their commerce. Carondelet, in reply to Trudeau's request for permission to send more support, noted that with the outbreak of war between Spain and England (October 1796) he had already sent Carlos Howard with troops and reinforcements to attend to the matter in accordance with his instructions.

The government of Spain respected Todd's grant, and when Julien Dubuque applied for a land grant in the area, it was first sent to Todd for approval. Then, in accordance with Todd's memorandum, the grant was made (to Dubuque), but trade was reserved to Todd. Todd was favored in nearly every way. He was given the exclusive right to supply all merchandise to Clamorgan, Loisel and Company and the former Missouri Company in spite of opposition from some members of the latter.

In November 1796, all hopes in Todd died, with him, when he fell victim to the yellow fever epidemic in New Orleans. Despite Clamorgan's intention to carry on Todd's work, Trudeau gave up all hope of Spain's permanent acquisition of the Indian trade of the Upper Mississippi Valley.

IV

British officials, especially at Michilimackinac and Detroit, protested against some of the Spaniards' activities. Louis Grignon, a resident at Prairie du Chien working for British interests, insisted that the British and Prairie du Chien feared Spaniards more than Americans. But by 1795 the situation had changed considerably. The Spaniards had initiated action against British instrusion; Spain and the United States had signed the Treaty of San Lorenzo el Real. Spain, who had been allied with the British against the French, had signed the Treaty of Basle in November 1795, and was currently aligned with France. War between England and Spain became probable, and actually did break out in October 1796. Despite the treaty between Spain and the United States in 1795, the Spaniards feared American penetration of southern Louisiana, attacks upon Upper Louisiana from the British in Canada, and they worried about French activities in the western parts of the United States. The fear was often mutual, for the British were concerned about Spanish attacks on Canada, as well as about the activities of the French in the West.

Since the creation of the United States, the young republic had had to fight for its very existence against the impressive power of England, Spain, and France, who intrigued to control the destiny, if not the territory, of the United States. Although both England and Spain held real estate, influence, and power in the Trans-Appalachia West, the young United States was able to capitalize on Europe's distress and achieve some notable success, at least on paper, in Jay's and Pinckney's treaties. The first, concluded in 1794 between the United States and Great Britain, was basically a commercial treaty. While it allowed the British complete navigation of the Mississippi, it also provided for the evacuation of the British from the Northwest posts. The second, concluded in 1795 between the United States and Spain, confirmed American ownership of land east of the Mississippi.

But by far the most threatening intrigues were those of the French. France's Minister P. A. Adet sent General George Victor Collot to gather intelligence about the west in an attempt to regain French influence and real estate in the Mississippi Valley. It was Collot who discovered and disclosed an intended British invasion from Canada and furnished information to Spanish envoy Carlos Martínez de Yrujo. In notes to the Spanish Minister, Collot detailed projected British attacks on the Spanish possessions of St. Louis, New Orleans, and Santa Fe. This was William Blount's conspiracy, tied in with land speculation, western adventurous intrigues, and other elements, which would have disturbed the entire Mississippi Valley. British complicity was evident, despite denials. American activities added to Spanish suspicions that Americans would aid British attacks on Spanish territory. Indeed, the discovery of the conspiracy prompted Spanish officials to fear aggression by the United States instead of by England. New Orleans was proposed as a second Gibraltar, and St. Louis was strongly manned. General Collot himself advanced plans for strengthening the defenses of Spanish St. Louis. The existence of a state of war between England and Spain constituted the ultimate anxiety for officials in Spanish Louisiana as well as in Spanish Illinois. The Spanish Court had declared war on England on the pretext that the English had established trading companies and posts on the Missouri with the intention of penetrating to the South Sea.

The Spanish sought to secure the area and centered defenses in Lower Louisiana. From Upper Louisiana they sent the trader Tesson Honoré to observe and counteract British traders among the

Indians of the Iowa country. They dispatched galliots up the Mississippi, supported by voluntary militia stationed opposite the mouth of the Illinois River, to warn of British activities. And they smuggled spies into Canada and the United States to collect both supplies and information.

While the Spanish in Louisiana were in constant fear of an English attack, the English were concerned with defection of the French habitants of Canada, and a possible Franco-Spanish attack on the Great Lakes posts. The Spaniards accomplished little toward enlisting French support in Upper Canada, but the French intrigues in Lower Canada were sufficient in themselves to affect British policy. French agents were traveling throughout Canada attempting to incite a rebellion. Fear of the Spaniards in the impending war prompted the British Ministry to take steps to defend both Upper and Lower Canada. The British scrutinized news from St. Louis and watched Spanish activities among the Indians closely. By the time Whitehall was finally convinced of the danger, and authorization for military preparations and stores was received in Upper Canada, the Spaniards had retired to Lower Louisiana to face the Americans; and the British became more concerned with peace overtures.

Collot and Adet, Yrujo and the Spaniards, Robert Liston, British minister to the U.S., and the Blount conspiracy—all of these and more kept the pot boiling from 1796 to 1804 in both Upper Canada and Upper Louisiana.

The activities of Spanish naval war vessels on the Upper Mississippi is but one highly important aspect of the events occurring along Anglo-Spanish frontier in the last decade of Spanish domination in the Mississippi Valley. The patrol was one of the chief Spanish means in defending the Mississippi frontier and represented a novel undertaking in eighteenth-century Louisiana.

It was natural to use armed war vessels to patrol the Gulf Coast and protect the mouths of the Mississippi River, but to attempt to use such vessels on the river itself was daring, especially above New Orleans. Such a maneuver—that is, a war flotilla of gunboats—was suggested as early as 1787. Although thought impossible, some of the heavier gunboats actually went up the river to New Madrid in 1793 and reached as far as St. Louis shortly thereafter. Lighter craft galliots, penetrated to Prairie du Chien and, in the last years of the century, even to the St. Peter's or Minnesota River. It is the galliots with which I shall deal here.

At the time of the formation of His Majesty's Light Squadron of Galleys in 1792, the fleet was composed of five galleys, two galliots, and one *lancha cañonera*. Shortly thereafter a heavy galley and two more galliots were added. The larger galleys carried thirty-two to thirty-four oars, as well as rather formidable armament; the crew consisted of a *patrón*, thirty-two to thirty-five sailors, and one proel. The smaller galleys carried about the same number of oars but lighter cannon. The galliots, *La Activa* and *La Flecha*, to be considered here, were reduced versions of the larger galleys, carrying fourteen to sixteen rowers and an armament of eight bronze swivel guns. This was the fleet that Spain had ready in the event of war.

Lieutenant-colonel Carlos Howard used the galliots in his 1796 expedition, and Lieutenant-governor Trudeau continued to use them on the Upper Mississippi to keep track of British and Indian activities. Although she did not effectively occupy her northern territory, Spain did attempt to control it, and keep others from occupying it on any permanent basis. Late in the 1790s, Spain's galliots were pressed into service, and aggressive plans laid to take control of the Indian trade along the Upper Missouri and Upper Mississippi rivers.

But Godoy's adage, that you cannot lock up an open field, applied. Spain's inability to send substantial reinforcements would result ultimately in failure. Pedro Cevallos wrote the following advice in his letter to the governor general of Louisiana on January 20, 1801: "try to carry on with those natives and with the United States in order not to compromise yourself; [proceed] with that care and tact prompted by a true zeal for the Royal service." "God and the Foreign Office" would protect the Spanish border provinces. Appealing to the deity was of scant comfort to the frightened officials of Louisiana, who needed the practical instruments of war. To control the trade and territory under their jurisdiction in the Upper Mississippi Valley, they required more troops, more money, an adequate fleet of galleys, fewer mercantile restrictions, and greater flexibility in the administration of government.

In truth, Spain never took advantage of the great potential of her lands along the Upper Mississippi. Godoy's characterization effectively summarized Spain's official attitude of resignation and failure. Despite all of their efforts, the Spaniards were never able to drive the English traders from the Upper Mississippi Valley. The possibilities of trade were almost limitless, but while the English were purchasing between 200,000 and 250,000 pounds worth of furs a year, the Spanish were buying only a very small fraction of that.

In 1801, Juan Manuel de Salcedo took office as the last Spanish governor of Louisiana. Jacques Clamorgan, as usual whenever a new governor took office, attempted to take advantage of the situation and requested governmental aid. He had had no success with Sebastián Calvo de la Puerta y O'Farrill (Marquis de Casa Calvo), the ad-interim governor who preceded Salcedo. Clamorgan called particular attention to the British monopoly of the Indian trade of the Upper Mississippi and Upper Missouri, and their influence on the Omaha Indians, who were preventing the Spaniards from ascending the Missouri. The English were subsidizing the Omaha, he maintained, and had invited them to a council in Prairie du Chien. As proof, he submitted that he had seen a copy of the journal of that council, which clearly revealed English intrigues. As a result, Clamorgan begged for one hundred militiamen and the privilege of exclusive trade rights with the Kansas and Platte river Indians. He got both. At the same time, Bernard Pratte procured the exclusive trade of the Des Moines River and built a fort at the mouth.

La Activa and *La Flecha* were still on the Upper Mississippi, but both were in sad condition. Henri Peyroux de la Coudrenière, commandant at New Madrid requested more galliots, as the American moves seemed ominous. *La Flecha* made regular voyages up the Mississippi, first under the command of Bernardo Molina and later under Santiago de St. Vrain. The latter ascended the river in 1801 and 1802, an exciting voyage that resulted in a confrontation at Prairie du Chien. But St. Vrain found the British traders and Indians too strong, and he was never able to penetrate as far as the St. Peter's River.

Although some Spanish traders worked the Iowa country, all Spanish efforts to prevent foreign trade with the Indians under their jurisdiction were futile; its laws in the area were a dead letter. Finally, on March 9, 1804, Carlos Dehault Delassus, lieutenant-governor at St. Louis, ordered the hoisting of the flag on *La Flecha*. The territory was transferred to the Americans, and the inventory of the *La Flecha* was made and shipped downriver. *La Flecha* was useless for transporting the regular Spanish inventory of arms and other materials. Yet, according to the record of payments, Santiago de St. Vrain remained in command of the inventory and received his salary, gratification, and rations until the end of April 1805, when he was considered detached from the service. When Delassus finally left St. Louis with the Spanish materials in November 1804, St. Vrain was in command of the boats.

Although the Spanish Fresh Water Navy was not strongly represented in Upper Louisiana after 1797, it played no small part in the regulation of commerce, Indian Affairs, communications, and defensive measures. That all Spanish activities in the Upper Mississippi, including valiant efforts utilizing the galliots, failed to remove foreign competition from Spanish-claimed territory, should not be surprising. Indeed, it was only after the War of 1812 that the Americans, then masters and owners of the territory, finally rousted the English from the Upper Mississippi Valley.

4

Before Lewis and Clark:
The Frontier along the Missouri

Despite Spanish attempts to reserve for their own subjects the territory, trade, influence, and loyalty of the Indians belonging to Spain under international law, intrepid and materialistically inclined Scotch traders, well supported by their British government and equally well capitalized, steadily encroached upon Spanish territory. Rich treasures in furs from the upper reaches of the Mississippi and Missouri valleys, as well as the more distant precious metals of New Spain, were an irresistable attraction to the enterprising British and Scotch traders from Canada. From Montreal, Detroit, Michilimackinac, Prairie du Chien, and the Lake of the Woods, British merchandise was carried by resourceful British traders deep into Spanish domain. Not only were the British agents aggressive, but they carried with them desirable, superior goods available at very reasonable prices. British traders were also British agents, and they were backed in their penetrations of Spanish territory by a trade-conscious home government. Hence the great bulk of furs extracted from the upper valleys, above the Des Moines and Platte rivers, found their way to the Great Lakes posts rather than to Spanish New Orleans.

In marked contrast, the profits-starved merchants of the Spanish posts were neglected, hampered, and bound by the rigidity of their own government. Although anxious for wealth and for domination of the Indian tribes, Spain adhered to classical mercantilism. The outmoded Spanish economic system was already crushed under a great weight of taxes, poor merchandise highly priced, involved, complicated, and expensive transportation routes, a cumbersome organization, and a paternalistic hierarchy. To these ills must be added the evils of nepotism, graft, inefficiency, ignorance, and shortsightedness.

66

Left to their own devices, the Spaniards of the Mississippi Valley were unable to maintain their advantage in the struggle with the British. Therefore it was not surprising that at the close of the American Revolution, the Spanish traders had not only lost their trade east of the Mississippi River, but also that within territory distinctly under their own jurisdiction, west of the river.

Spain had the difficult task of defending a long frontier line and an immense territory against an aggressive and well-equipped rival. The province could expect neither troops nor aid from the decadent court of Charles IV. Furthermore the Americans were also becoming a menace to Spanish sovereignty by the surge of their westward movement, and the insidious propaganda of the French Revolution undermined absolute authority throughout Spanish America. As revealed in chapter three, the situation was critical indeed in the last decade of the eighteenth century. Under Governor Esteban Miró at New Orleans and his lieutenant-governor at St. Louis, Manuel Pérez, half-hearted and time-worn methods were applied for the relief of this desperate situation.

Thus the British acquired complete domination over the Indians and trade in the Upper Mississippi Valley west of the Mississippi, while to the east the Anglo-Spanish rivalry became an Anglo-American rivalry and quarrel. The Americans had a difficult time and did not resolve the problems successfully until long after the acquisition of Louisiana, the expedition of Zebulon Montgomery Pike, and the War of 1812.

Once the British secured economic control of the Upper Mississippi Valley, they pushed relentlessly towards the Missouri and beyond. British traders not only reached the Missouri from Michilimackinac and Prairie du Chien, they also began to push westward on the trail first blazed by the La Vérendrye family in 1738-39. Traders from the posts of Hudson's Bay Company and the Northwest Company in Canada began to turn southward in a fierce struggle to extend commercial relations. They succeeded in developing a lucrative trade with the Mandan Indians, whose home was located near the northern "Big Bend" in the Missouri River.

The frontier of Spanish Louisiana shifted to the Missouri, where again the Spaniards made a heroic effort to keep effective hold of the territory to its west and to establish a defensive northeastern and northern frontier along the vast extent of the Viceroyalty of New Spain. This was, in effect, not only because the Indian trade, which by right was Spanish, was being taken away from them, but also because of the threat to Spanish control of the Provincias Internas and even New Spain.

From yet another direction came threats, if not actual encroachments, upon Spanish territory. The Russians were descending southward along the Pacific coast from Alaskan bases. The British had been active for some time in the waters of the North Pacific and on the northwest coast of North America, while Americans in increaing numbers were beginning to show up in the same area. The resulting "Swirl of the Nations" ended in the famous Nootka Sound episode, as a result of which Spain was forced to surrender her exclusive claim to the territory lying along the western shore of North America above the forty-second parallel. To protect herself against these two lines of approach—the Russians from the north and the British moving westward and southward—Spain was forced to ascend the Missouri, in the hope of finding a direct passageway to the Western Sea. The Russians continued to push southward, and fear of their encroachment upon California, now a valued Spanish possession, was expressed by many Spanish officials. In the steady advance of the Canadian traders to the west and to the south, Spain perceived a direct threat to her New Mexican and Pacific possessions. The best possible means of protecting the Spanish possessions was to open a line of communication and establish a line of posts along the Missouri River highway, from St. Louis to the sea. By doing so, a fortified Upper Louisiana, still called Spanish Illinois country, would serve as a barrier to the advance both of the British and of the Russians, and at the same time defensively hem in and connect all the possessions of Spain in North America. Then the northeastern frontier of New Spain (Spanish Louisiana) would be secure. This was the dream of many a subject of His Catholic Majesty in the last decade of the eighteenth century. Spain made a heroic effort to achieve this security. It was, however, to be Lewis and Clark who brought that dream to reality shortly after the transfer of Louisiana to the United States, with the United States taking Spain's place in challenging the English for dominance of the Missouri Valley trade.

In 1792, with the assumption of office by the Baron de Carondelet in New Orleans, and Zenon Trudeau in St. Louis,

Spain launched a mighty push up the Missouri and to the west. Profit, economic gain, international rivalry, national pride and prestige, and frontier adventure combined to wipe out more of the geographical misinformation of the area, to connect the Mississippi posts with Santa Fe and the Pacific coast, and to establish an impenetrable chain of forts—a defensive fortified line protecting the patrimony of Spain in northern North America. Spain knew that she had to assume the offensive in order to preserve her empire. To oust the foreigner, to garner renewed profits, to gain the friendship of the Indians, to explore the domain, and to carry the Spanish flag to the uttermost limits of Spain's jurisdiction became the prime objectives of Lieutenant-governor Zenon Trudeau. What resulted was a series of Spanish expeditions in the closing years of the eighteenth century that reached from the Niobrara River to the forks of the Missouri.

Prior to 1790, the Spanish had made little progress up the Missouri River. In 1769, the Panimaha were the most distant tribe on record visited by the Spaniards, although isolated Spanish traders might have reached Indians beyond. Names of more distant Indian tribes were known only from hearsay. Under Lieutenant-governor Francisco Cruzat the Spaniards had gone no farther than the Niobrara River. Progress slackened during the American Revolution, since the Spanish had to concern themselves with defending the Mississippi. They confined their activities on the Missouri to keeping the loyalty of their Indians and preventing Indian outbreaks. The Spanish Illinois country suffered economically as a result. Some (Spanish) traders, however, were sent to the Missouri and in 1780 reaped a good profit. Esteban Miró warned Cruzat in 1785 to be especially vigilant concerning American intrusion into the Missouri trade and urged him to follow the earlier successful example of Pedro Piernas in keeping the English traders out of Spanish dominions (referring to the Ducharme case). Manuel Pérez, in 1788, reported that trade was brisk on the Missouri, but had to admit that the English traders were utilizing the Indians of the Mississippi as go-betweens in trading with the Missouri Indians for beaver and otter, the richest furs in the country.

That the geography of the Upper Missouri was largely unknown and grossly exaggerated is obvious in a Spanish account of Louisiana in 1785, submitted to the commandant general of the Provincias Internas by Miró. There was hardly an improvement

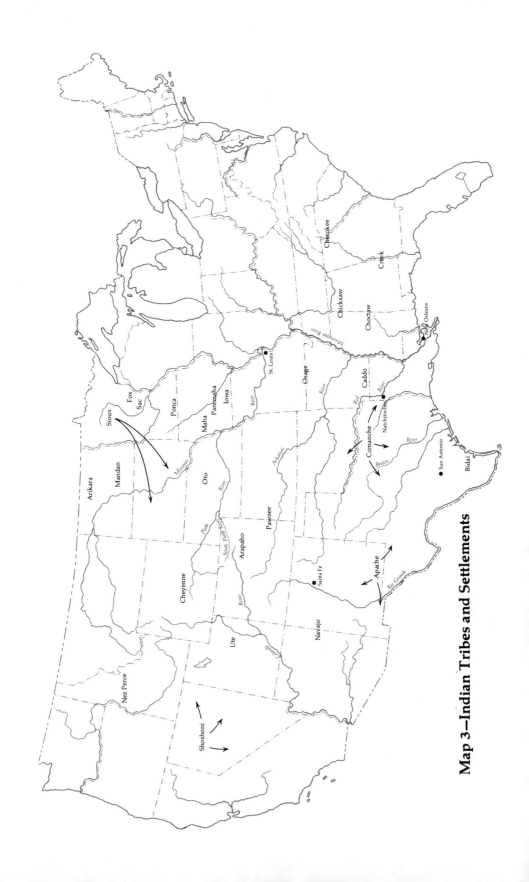

Map 3—Indian Tribes and Settlements

over French knowledge of the area dating from 1758. No one, said Miró, had been higher up than where the Sioux lived on the Missouri, although he mentioned the Arikara Indians who lived beyond. Miró's speculation amounted to giving an oversimplified picture of the Missouri-Platte rivers circling south-westward into the mountains and stretching close to the sources of the Río Bravo (Rio Grande). He based his information on that of traders at St. Louis. During the first twenty-five years of Spanish rule in Louisiana, the Spaniards had busied themselves developing their trade with neighboring tribes and fortifying their frontier against the encroachments of the British. But beginning about 1788, they were forced to ascend the Missouri. Manuel Pérez from St. Louis warned that the Americans and English had long looked for the means to penetrate the Missouri. "If war should break out," he observed, "the result would be the loss of the Missouri country, which would inaugurate an epoch of vagabonds penetrating the province of New Mexico and pillaging the mines." Diego de Gardoqui, Spain's chargé d'affaires, wrote from Philadelphia of enthusiastic Englishmen who had been in territory belonging to His Catholic Majesty. One of the Englishmen, who had visited the Upper Mississippi and Missouri as far as the mountains, had met Indians who had told him of a river flowing westward into the Pacific Ocean. He even had a map of it. Gardoqui also learned of Lord Edward Fitzgerald's plans to cross the wilderness to Mexico. Gardoqui pleaded for Spanish reconnaissance of the sources of the rivers flowing to the west as far as the Pacific Ocean.

In most correspondence and speeches, Spanish Illinois was described as the key to Mexico, making it advisable, if not imperative, to build forts on the Missouri, Des Moines, and St. Peter's rivers in order to thwart the aggressive British. The English traders on those rivers were plentiful and had an abundance of merchandise which they could, and did sell and exchange at cheaper prices than the Spaniards were able to. Moreover, merchandise was available to them, but not to the Spanish merchants. Paysá—the territory at the confluence of the Missouri and Mississippi rivers—was well-known for colonial projects of settlements, land speculation, and as a jumping off place for entering Spanish territory. The project of ascending the Missouri was speculated upon, and attempted by foreigners, such as Lieutenant John Armstrong, André Michaux, and others.

Moreover, during the Nootka Sound controversy, when war seemed imminent between Spain and England, Spanish officials feared a British invasion from Canada into the Spanish Illinois country with St. Louis as the principal objective. This came at a time when Spain's relations with the recently installed government of the United States were far from cordial. Spain feared that the United States would grant permission to England to cross the newly organized Northwest Territory in order to carry out her projected attack against Spain's Mississippi Valley possessions. That permission, although perhaps never officially requested, was discussed in Washington's cabinet, a maneuver rather definitely aimed at forcing Spain's diplomatic hand in her relations with the United States. Alexander Hamilton, for example, favored such action if a sufficiently attractive quid pro quo could be obtained.

For some years the Spaniards traded regularly with the Indians of the Missouri—at least as far as the Maha. In 1791, Manuel Pérez spoke of Oto Indians who had gone to trade with the English establishments on the Mississippi, and observed that traders from that area were going as far as the Missouri to trade with the Indians. Pérez then reiterated his suggestion of forts at the mouths of the Des Moines and St. Peter's rivers to prevent the infiltration of the English smugglers.

Pérez' successor, Zenon Trudeau, was instructed to maintain peace and good harmony with the English and the Americans, although at that time the Americans were considered dangerous to Spanish dominions. He was strictly enjoined not to permit traders, even English ones, in territory of His Catholic Majesty. The Indians also continued to present problems. With their defeat of Arthur St. Clair, governor of U. S. Northwest Territory, in 1791, they became so excited and so emboldened that some of them even threatened Spanish territory. Part of the Indians' courage was based on British promises of support. The troubles the Spaniards had with the Osage complicated the situation even more. Depriving the Osage of goods and declaring war on them could throw them into the lap of the English.

When Carondelet assumed office he decreed that the trade of the Missouri be open to all subjects of His Catholic Majesty. This was contrary to the previous policy of trade only by license. Trudeau, who dutifully published the decree, nevertheless exercised some control in the issuance of licenses to trade. In 1793, Trudeau wrote a lengthy report about English trade, the superiority of English commerce over that of Spain, and listed places where the canoes of the English from Michilimackinac wintered for trade with the Indians. Therein he noted that traders entered Spanish territory from Prairie du Chien and from Rivière Pomme de Terre via the St. Peter's River, and that trading with Sioux they went to the Upper Missouri. Along the Des Moines they had established trade with the Pawnee and Maha; and along the Iowa and others they traded among the Indians of Iowa-Minnesota (in present Nebraska and the Dakotas).

Requested by Carondelet to acquire more information concerning the Mandan Indians, Trudeau replied on May 20, 1793, that he was unable to comply with his request; that he had consulted Jacques D'Eglise, first Spaniard to reach the Mandan on the Upper Missouri, but had found that "discoverer" simpleminded and not a keen observer. Trudeau expressed the hope that within a few days he would be in contact with a well-informed Canadian *mozo* who had been among the Mandan, while in the employ of the English company. Trudeau also stated that some hunters from St. Louis had penetrated to the Mandan that year, and upon their return he felt he would be able to obtain and transmit more information. Thus the Spanish began a new period of activity in the Missouri River region, undertaken from St. Louis. An increasing number of (Spanish) traders from St. Louis began to crowd into the trade among the known tribes in the Lower Missouri Valley. They also spread out in search of new contacts and new markets. Several examples are available.

In 1789, Juan (Jean Baptiste) Meunier, a Spanish trader, claimed that he had discovered the Ponca tribe living on the Niobrara River and had obtained from the government the exclusive right to trade with those Indians. (His claim to the discovery of the Poncas was later proved false.) He later conveyed or sold that right to Jacques Clamorgan. Shortly thereafter, two new names entered the chronicle of the Spanish advance up the Missouri. In 1787, Joseph Garreau, a hunter, was sent to trap and hunt on the Upper Missouri, although nothing of his accomplishments has come to light as yet.

In August 1790, Jacques D'Eglise obtained a license to hunt on the Missouri. In his meanderings, he became the first Spanish subject to reach the Mandan and Tayenne Indian villages eight hundred leagues from the mouth of the Missouri. The English were already there. D'Eglise reported that he found a Frenchman named Menard, who had been living among the Mandan for fourteen years. He also noted that the Mandan were in constant communication with the British, who had established posts only fifteen days to the north (on the Assiniboine). The Kiowa, whose home was still in present South Dakota, so it seems, were intermediaries between the Englishmen on the Upper Missouri and the Spaniards of New Mexico. In fact, D'Eglise saw Spanish saddles and bridles among the Mandan. D'Eglise persuaded the Mandan of the greatness of the Spanish government and promised that he would establish trade. Returning to St. Louis, he reported all this to Trudeau. When Carondelet received the information, he told Trudeau that he was acquainted with the information and desired more extensive data on the Mandan.

D'Eglise had returned from his trip in October 1792. He set out again, accompanied by Garreau and goods in March 1793. The Sioux and Arikara prevented the two men from reaching the Mandan. As a result, Garreau remained among the Arikara. D'Eglise returned and asked for the exclusive right to trade with the Mandan. This he did not receive, for the newly formed Missouri Company had already been given that right.

The information garnered from D'Eglise and others concerning the British among the Mandan, and of interchange, through Indian go-betweens, with the Spaniards of New Mexico, filled the Spanish officials of Louisiana with alarm. The competition of the British traders along the western shore of the Mississippi River was being felt; the Indian trade of the Lower Missouri, still controlled by the Spaniards, was dwindling. Whereas Spanish profits of one hundred to three hundred percent had once been common, in 1793 the trade had so diminished that traders had to be satisfied with a profit of twenty-five percent. There were, in fact, too many traders for the small number of Indian tribes with whom the Spaniards were actually in contact. Trade had to be expanded and the British had to be taught to respect international boundary lines. To implement both these aims, one course of action was imperative: ascend the Missouri, establish an acquaintance with the new tribes, and wrest the trade from the British. Even if there existed no chance for pecuniary gain, the Indians might be persuaded to oppose, if not actually attack, the British. It seemed to Spanish officials that fear and loss of money might soon discourage

Canadian traders from crossing the Anglo-Spanish frontier. Without doubt the activities of Jacques D'Eglise had inspired trader and official alike to enact the final scene in the drama of Spain's dominion in the Spanish Illinois.

In an effort to make the trade of the Illinois country more lucrative, Carondelet in 1792 decreed that all Spanish subjects might participate, subject only to the restriction of obtaining permission (license) from the lieutenant-governor. However, such unrestricted freedom could not last for any length of time. Jealousies and competition brought adverse results, and rivalry between subjects of the same government led to bad conduct. The merchants of St. Louis soon complained that the Indians of the Missouri were being corrupted by the abundant low-priced merchandise of the English. They wanted the trade restricted to Spanish subjects—merchants, traders, and others who would not violate Spanish regulations. Carondelet thus followed up his proclamation granting free trade with a set of rules to regulate trade in the Illinois country. Trade with the Missouri tribes was to be divided among the merchants of St. Louis by lot; a year's residence in Upper Louisiana and business with a New Orleans firm were prerequisites for obtaining a license; foreigners were excluded, even in cases of employees. The merchants had to ratify the regulations, and elect a syndic to enforce them. This they did, then immediately asked for permission to organize expeditions to confiscate the goods of foreigners trading in Spanish territory. One half of the confiscated materials was to go to members of the expedition, and one half to the "association" to defray the expenses incurred by the group. Here was a first intimation of economic combining with patriotic motive to achieve the double objective of private pecuniary gain and defense of the Spanish realm. To further their aims, the merchants of St. Louis requested permission to form a company which would have exclusive trading privileges with all the Indian nations of the Missouri which the company might discover, visit, or obtain information about above the Ponca. Moreover, to increase their profits and facilitate their trade, the company asked for the privilege of purchasing goods in time of war from the British or the Americans because of the scarcity of merchandise in Spanish Illinois.

It was Jacques Clamorgan who now stepped into the picture. He was an experienced slave dealer, fur trader, merchant, financier, and land speculator, endowed with a tremendous imagination, and

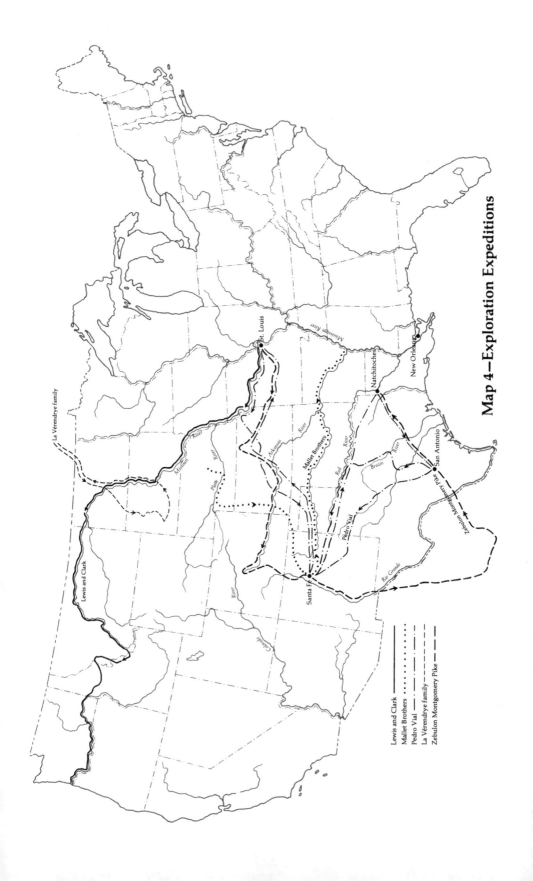

Map 4—Exploration Expeditions

Lewis and Clark ········
Mallet Brothers ·········
Pedro Vial —·—·—·—
La Vérendrye family — — —
Zebulon Montgomery Pike — — — —

a glib tongue. Although never married, he was the father of four children. He had rather recently come to Upper Louisiana. He was respected but not accepted socially by the aristocratic French creoles of the province. This was less a reflection upon his charming personality than upon his well-stocked harem of colored beauties. He was known to be an intriguer and at times his probity was somewhat questioned. Usually he was found to be pliant and even servile, but he was accustomed to conducting great operations. He seldom failed to get what he wanted from the Spanish officials; if not directly, then indirectly. He was to become known in Louisiana as a statesman, an explorer, and a promoter. Clamorgan was in many ways the precursor of Lewis and Clark. He traversed Texas, and engaged in the Santa Fe trade, long before his successors made those trails famous. This island creole managed his affairs in such a way that even his enemies (and they were not few in number) could not fail to recognize his talents.

Clamorgan quickly became the leader of the merchants. His ability to put vast dreams onto paper, and persuade all of their validity, was enviable. He was elected syndic and thus represented the merchants of St. Louis. Soon he became the driving force behind the movement to restore commerce in the Spanish Illinois and to regain for the King of Spain real sovereignty over the Spanish dominions of the Mississippi Valley. It was Clamorgan who suggested the formation of the renowned Company of Discoverers and Explorers of the Missouri. This "Missouri Company" was formed for the purpose of ousting the British traders from Spanish territory; of capturing the trade with the Indians; of discovering a route to the Pacific and joining the Missouri country with Mexico and California; of defending the Spanish empire along its undefended and unexplored northernmost frontier; and of protecting strategic and rich Santa Fe.

Clamorgan persuaded a number of merchants of Illinois to take part in the Company. Although he was but one of nine members of the Company, it was Clamorgan who became the director and managed its bold schemes, usually products of his fertile imagination. In carrying them out, he succeeded in financially ruining not only himself, but his associates. The articles of incorporation were drawn up, signed, and sent by Trudeau (who approved them) to Carondelet on May 31, 1794. The latter quickly approved and sent them off to Spain. The government of Spain did not formally approve the formation of the company until 1796, when company fortunes were already on the decline.

The Missouri Company sent three costly expeditions up the Missouri to drive the British from Spanish territory, develop the valuable trade in the Upper Missouri Valley, and discover a route to the Pacific. In search of the last, Carondelet offered a prize of three thousand dollars to the first person to reach the South Sea via the Missouri River. Many, among them D'Eglise, tried for the prize. The resultant surge of activity did not succeed in opening a route to the ocean nor did it effectively close the area to the British. As a matter of fact, the Spaniards had difficulty penetrating the Upper Missouri above the Pawnee and north of the Platte River because of the ever present influence of British goods and traders upon the Indians, who harassed the Spaniards in their voyages up the Missouri. A few did succeed in penetrating the Upper Missouri, but the same conditions prevailed as late as 1804 and 1807, when the Lewis and Clark and the Nathaniel Pryor and Manuel Lisa expeditions experienced the very same difficulties in the Upper Missouri region. The records of the Lewis and Clark expedition especially reveal the extent of British effectiveness and control of the trade with the Upper Missouri Valley Indians. The British were so well-entrenched that even infighting, like that between the Hudson's Bay and Northwest Companies, for the trade of the same Indian nations did not destroy that control.

The Company's expeditions to the Upper Missouri proved to be costly failures. The first, under the former schoolmaster Jean Baptiste Truteau, failed to reach above the Arikara. However, it contributed greatly to expanding the geographical knowledge of the Spaniards, and to acquaintances with other Indians, principally the Shoshoni tribes on the Yellowstone. As a result of the information gathered by Truteau, the Missouri became fairly well-known as far as the mouth of the Yellowstone. The second expedition under a trader named Lecuyer was a fiasco; his expedition in 1795 was expected to reach the Pacific Ocean shores by the spring of 1796. Obviously, it did not.

One of the reasons for Truteau's failure was interference by Jacques D'Eglise who, despite urgings by Zenon Trudeau, refused to join the Missouri Company. Instead, he organized his own group and started up the Missouri to the Mandan. Traveling lighter and more swiftly, D'Eglise overtook Truteau, reached the Arikara first, and reaped the benefits of the fur trade with those Indians. D'Eglise then returned to St. Louis together with two Canadian traders, arriving on July 4, 1795.

The two Canadians, Juan Fotman and Chrysostome Joncquard, were carefully questioned by Zenon Trudeau. From them a great deal of information concerning British activities on the Upper Missouri, as well as some geographical knowledge, was gained. In addition, it was learned that for some time a direct trade had been carried on with the Mandan by the Canadian traders, who had even built a fort on the Missouri. Trudeau also learned that the Mandan, Gros Ventre, and other nearby Indian nations were in communication with the Spaniards situated to the south. This new information, and the expiration of Truteau's contract with the Company, served as the impetus for the greatest surge of Spanish effort up the Missouri.

James Mackay—Scotsman turned Spanish subject—honest, able, and prudent, was given a large and costly expedition, launched in 1795, to open commerce with the distant and unknown nations on the upper reaches of the Missouri, and to discover all the unknown parts of His Catholic Majesty's dominions as far as the Pacific Ocean. Replacing Truteau as company agent, he was ordered to construct posts, in order to protect Spanish trade from the British intruders; further he was to serve as commandant of such forts from which he was to launch attacks on British forts and drive them from the Mandan. Although he experienced difficulties with the Indians, he did build Fort Charles among the Omaha Indians near the mouth of the Platte River. Mackay himself never got much further north, although he did valuable service in Nebraska and on the Platte. But to fulfill his assignment, he commissioned his trusted "lieutenant," the Welshman John Evans, to continue up the river, cross the mountains, discover the sources of the Missouri and a passage to the Pacific Ocean. Mackay's instructions to Evans followed the wishes of Clamorgan, director of the Company, under the protection of Governor-general Carondelet and Lieutenant-governor Trudeau. A journal was to be kept, Spanish ownership and Missouri Company control asserted, and friendship of the Indians obtained. Evans was directed to keep within the bounds of forty degrees north latitude until he arrived in the area between one hundred and eleven and one hundred and twelve degrees longitude, west, then he was to travel north to the forty-second parallel and thence due west. The distance from the Rocky Mountains to the Pacific Ocean, Mackay estimated at two hundred and ninety leagues.

Evans reached the Mandan, asserted Spanish control, and presented English traders of the Hudson's Bay and Northwest Companies with copies of Spanish orders to get out of Spanish territory. He hauled down the British flag, raised the Spanish colors, destroyed the British fort among the Mandan, and harangued the Indians. Yet he stopped the British only temporarily. Evans also failed to reach the Pacific shores. But the efforts of Mackay and Evans resulted in new maps of the Missouri and of vastly increased information about the Indian nations of the Upper Missouri.

Despite the failure of Mackay and Evans to reach the Western Sea, Spanish zeal for the enterprise was not altogether lost. Jacques Clamorgan, for one, was still vitally interested. Although he had ruined himself in the Company, he made use of the competing jealousies of the merchants, and by cleverly rewriting the articles of incorporation, he acquired all but one of the original shares. In the name of the Company, he petitioned successfully for large land grants and new trading privileges. Eventually these holdings came into his own hands. Whenever any individual, and there were many, asked the government for trade privileges which would endanger his hold on things, Clamorgan not only successfully opposed them but usually won these identical concessions for the Company and for himself. Those who continued to oppose the Company found themselves controlled by virtue of Clamorgan's superior ability to advance and furnish merchandise.

Clamorgan befriended François Régis Loisel and, more important for a time at least, the wealthy British merchant, Andrew Todd. Backed by the wealth, reputation, and recognized ability of Todd, Clamorgan plunged ahead. He persuaded the Spanish officials to give Todd the exclusive right of trade in the Upper Missouri Valley. This was later extended to include the Sac and Fox trade. Todd was also granted a reduction of import and export duties and other commercial concessions. Clamorgan persuaded Carondelet to grant further exclusive grants of trade to the Missouri Company as well as a subsidy of ten thousand pesos for one hundred militiamen who were to guard forts which Clamorgan planned to establish along a great arc reaching from the Mississippi River to the Pacific Ocean. He got a commission for Mackay as captain of these forts. Clamorgan further convinced Carondelet to make important changes in the bylaws of the Missouri Company so that Todd, excluded as a foreigner, could receive an equal share in the Company. Permission for the Company to buy exclusively through Todd for a commission was also granted. Thus, despite opposition of the other merchants of St. Louis, Clamorgan established a monopoly on the Indian trade in both the Upper Missouri and Upper Mississippi valleys. To exploit these advantages and to press for more, Clamorgan formed Clamorgan, Loisel and Company, which asked for the concessions not ceded to or permitted by the Missouri Company. Clamorgan thus acted in a dual capacity as director of both companies.

Clamorgan succeeded in this enterprise, in part because he appeared to have the full backing of Todd's resources, and in part because the governor was most anxious to oust the British from Spanish domain and to establish a route to the Pacific Ocean. But when Todd died in 1796, his heirs and creditors besieged St. Louis and New Orleans to get all they could. They made no effort to continue Todd's enterprise or to fulfill his contracts. This was the one time that Clamorgan overshot his mark. He was heavily indebted to the Briton, whose heirs and agents forced Clamorgan to the brink of bankruptcy.

By sheer personality, long flattering letters, and visits to New Orleans, Clamorgan managed somehow to retain all of the Company concessions. In fact, he gained more. He was bold enough to propose continuing efforts to defend the Spanish empire and to discover a route to the Pacific, even in the face of financial ruin. Even Trudeau supported him because, when pressed, Clamorgan's creditors found no one to testify against him. Trudeau also realized that if Clamorgan's creditors foreclosed on him it would ruin many of the inhabitants of St. Louis. Even Clamorgan's former opponents, Daniel Clark in New Orleans and Auguste Chouteau in St. Louis, came to his rescue.

Yet Clamorgan's gains were only temporary. With the accession of weak governors after the untimely death of Gayoso de Lemos in 1799, the Company began to lose ground. Clamorgan's opponents began to get trading rights previously reserved for the Company. The British were greatly strengthened on the Upper Missouri and were descending as far as the Omaha. And on the Mississippi, the British usurped the trade north of St. Louis.

Clamorgan hung on, backed by Lieutenant-Governor Carlos Dehault Delassus and extended credit by Daniel Clark, a New Orleans merchant. He first sent Hugh Heney, a fur trader, to discover the route to the Pacific, but Heney was thwarted by the British. Clamorgan obtained the speculative trade of the Oto, Ponca, and Maha Indians, and the sure and profitable Kansa trade. He renewed his request for ten thousand pesos, one hundred militiamen, and two thousand pounds of gunpowder. In this he was also thwarted.

Stripped of all trades except that of the Pani, Clamorgan resorted to backing the efforts of others. He obtained a one-third interest in the Loisel-Heney contract. In this way Clamorgan's plans for the Spanish frontier were carried on until the American occupation of Louisiana. While another thrust was made toward the Pacific, Clamorgan descended to New Orleans to solicit aid from the government, to arrange his affairs, and to resolve conflicting exclusive grants. Once again he did well. He received from the government support for the Missouri Company. Once again he was to promote resistance to British aggression. He was granted the exclusive trade of the entire Missouri Valley, except that with the Kansa Indians; and he probably backed Santiago (Jacques) Chauvin, a St. Louis merchant who received that trade. Even Delassus was ordered to support Clamorgan as director of the Company.

Clamorgan gave backing to nearly all of the experienced men in the Upper Missouri. In 1802, in order to engage in Indian trade, D'Eglise obtained thirty-eight thousand pesos worth of merchandise from Clamorgan, obligating himself to pay for it in the spring of 1803. He also secured a passport from Trudeau permitting him to trade in the Missouri. D'Eglise was to explore to the Pacific and perhaps to Santa Fe as well. Clamorgan, Loisel and Company actually led the activities on the Upper Missouri, keeping in mind Clamorgan's schemes to establish Spanish dominion throughout that vast area. And Clamorgan, now even supported by his former enemies and competitors, used Loisel's work as a basis for acquiring more land grants from the Spanish officials.

The British, however, were extending their activities inexorably down the Missouri, activities claimed in October 1796 as a cause for

Spain's declaration of war on England. Despite the fact that for years Clamorgan, Loisel and Company had dispatched agents and merchandise to the Upper Missouri and particularly to the Mandan villages, British competition was having its effect. With equal persistence, but even more aggressiveness and success, British traders with headquarters in Prairie du Chien were spreading westward, virtually monopolizing the trade of the Iowa-Minnesota country. They now began to capture the Ponca and Omaha trade, having established posts not only in the Iowa country but on the Platte River as well. So successful were they that nearly every Company vessel sent up the Missouri was pillaged by British Indian allies. In 1800, Clamorgan petitioned Lieutenant-governor Delassus to grant him the privilege of building stations and forts along the Kansas and Platte rivers to afford protection for a new route to the Mandan villages, one that would avoid the villages of the Ponca and Omaha. He begged in vain for the one hundred militiamen that had been promised in 1796, and complained bitterly of the British destruction of Hugh Heney's expedition.

Many of the merchants of St. Louis received the trades of the nations of the Missouri but they themselves did not go out; instead traders supplied by them must have done so. D'Eglise certainly did, ascending the Mississippi in late 1803 or 1804. With the permission of the lieutenant-governor, André Cayouga and Company with goods supplied by Joseph Hortiz, a St. Louis merchant, probably traded on the Upper Missouri in 1802-03. Joseph H. Robidoux supplied other traders. Delassus said in 1803 that D'Eglise had been employed by Clamorgan and he assumed that he had gone to Mexico. The Marquis de Casa Calvo wrote that Laurent Durocher (Lorenzo Deroche) and Santiago (Jacques) D'Eglise had gone to the Upper Missouri to facilitate communication with Santa Fe, and since he had not returned that year (1804) he presumed that he had penetrated into New Mexico. This, in point of fact, D'Eglise did, reaching Santa Fe in 1805. Heney was operating continually in the Upper Missouri as were Loisel and Pierre-Antoine Tabeau.

Fear of the invasion of Spanish territory from the north, and dread of British and American penetration to New Mexico, was constant throughout this period. This fear stemmed particularly from the general belief that the Missouri took its rise in the mountains, from which spot it would be a relatively easy task to descend to New Mexico. The Spanish were especially alarmed in 1804 when several traders led by Baptiste La Lande and equipped at the expense of William Morrison of Kaskaskia, then the richest and most enterprising merchant in the west, were dispatched to Santa Fe.

In New Mexico, Governor Joaquín del Real Alencaster attempted, or at least desired to use D'Eglise and those traders who had followed him (as Spanish subjects), to bind the friendship of the Indian nations inhabiting the banks of the Missouri River from its confluence with the Platte westward. They did accompany Pedro Vial and Juan Chalvert (also appearing in documents as José Calvert, Jarvay, Jarvet) on an expedition to the Pawnee as interpreters. Several other "Frenchmen" reached Santa Fe from the Missouri and many others followed.

From the activities and reports of Régis Loisel and Pierre-Antoine Tabeau, who later wrote the narrative of Loisel's expedition and who had spent several years in the Upper Missouri, Spanish officials learned how easily the British might travel by water, "with the exception of a couple of portages," from Hudson's Bay to the mountains surrounding Santa Fe. Delassus reported that the Platte River took its rise but a short distance west of Santa Fe, and that although it was not navigable the whole distance, travel overland was easy and open to Americans who wished to reach New Mexico. Foreigners could also go to New Mexico via the Cheyenne and the Yellowstone rivers. The most effective means of preventing such penetrations was to befriend the Indians along these routes and set them against British and American intruders. Casa Calvo even proposed that Loisel be appointed as Indian agent with his main work that of restricting the entrance of aliens into Spanish territory.

The data from Loisel proved true shortly afterwards. But in the meantime Spain's hold on the territory immediately west of the Mississippi ended abruptly. The Corsican ruler of France, after wrangling that area from Spain, broke his promise and sold it to the United States. Immediately thereafter, President Jefferson dispatched Captains Lewis and Clark to carry out his pet project of exploring a route to the Pacific Ocean. The Spaniards had paved the way for this important achievement, and it is reasonable to assume that had Spain continued its rule in the Upper Mississippi Valley she too would have achieved this longstanding goal.

The Spanish borderland—the frontier of Spanish Louisiana—again receded. But the recession of that frontier and borderland was one of flag only; the area was not occupied until step by step the Spaniards were pushed back by the more aggressive British and Americans. Louisiana was sold to the United States, but boundaries became an important stumbling block. Spain claimed the Missouri River as its boundary; the United States claimed the territory to the Rocky Mountains. Britain, though she claimed nothing, managed to retain economic control in the disputed area. The new frontier of Spanish Louisiana—its last—was to be disputed until 1819 when it was finally settled by the Adams-Onís treaty. With the ratification of that treaty in 1821, Spanish rule would come to an end in North America.

5

The Road to Santa Fe:
Genesis of the Santa Fe Trail

Spain's unassailable power in the sixteenth century made it possible for rapid and extensive expansion in North America. Justifying its role on the basis of God, humanitarianism, and the more prosaic search for wealth, Spain rapidly colonized in Mexico and culminated its expansion in New Mexico. Yet in the following century, Spain found herself in a period of economic decline, and the rise of powerful rivals in Europe and America led to many intrusions upon the Spanish monopoly of North America. Throughout the eighteenth century—indeed until Spain's hasty departure from North America in the 1820s—the Indian problem plagued Spanish officialdom. Lieutenant colonel Antonio de Bonilla who was adjutant-inspector of the Provincias Internas, equated the defense of New Mexico with that of Mexico, and New Mexican officials were ordered to prevent foreign and Indian (Apache and Comanche) advances. But Spain, weakened and unable to defend its frontier adequately before such vigorous onslaughts, had to turn for help to the powerful Indian warriors of the Plains. To a very large degree Indian aid constituted Spain's defiance of European intruders. Fulfillment of French ambitions required passage over Indian territory; Spanish-Indian cooperation could close the highways leading to New Mexico. War and peace with the Indians became matters of national welfare. For one hundred and forty-five years the Spaniards kept New Mexico to themselves.

New Mexico revolved around Santa Fe, the seat of the provincial government. At first trouble occurred with the Pueblo Indians of

New Mexico but that passed with Spanish reconquest after the Pueblo Revolt of 1680.

To the southeast and northeast New Mexico was circled by a fierce ring. North were the fighting Comanche who had left their homes between the Yellowstone and Platte rivers and moved southward to the plains adjoining New Mexico. They began to harass Spanish New Mexico early in the eighteenth century. Northwest of the Comanche were the Ute; while southeast, south and southwest were the Apache, both groups that would plague the Spaniards.

The French edged westward from the Illinois area and Canada, and from New Orleans and the Mississippi. Such expansion prompted the Spanish, for defensive reasons, to occupy Texas lest it fall into French hands. Spain finally won the no-man's-land of Texas and established its capital of Los Adaes in western Louisiana. The French line of occupation stretched to Natchitoches, and competition for the Indians' good will and trade extended beyond. The French did get through to and across Texas, however, and found routes from Illinois to Santa Fe, as well as from New Orleans to Santa Fe, despite Spanish prohibitions and precautions. In these areas, powerful Indian nations fought French encroachments and aided Spanish defenses.

Despite royal court orders and official Spanish hostilities, Frenchmen continued their quest. The routes from Louisiana to New Mexico were well known by the mid-eighteenth century. Farther north the French overcame the trade barrier with New Mexico when the Comanche, after defeating the Apache, became the leading nation. The French went among the Comanche and on to Santa Fe. There had been contacts before but the Mallet brothers opened a trail to Santa Fe, and others soon followed. From Natchitoches, too, beginning with the Canadian trader Louis Juchereau de Saint-Denis, contact was made with New Mexico, and travel to Santa Fe as well as into Texas opened. Obstacles were many but the rewards more than compensated for the risks. When, under French protection, the Comanche were induced to sign a treaty (1746) with an old French ally, the Jumano Indians, a free route to New Mexico along the lower Arkansas River became available. The Spaniards sought peace with the Comanche without success, and more Frenchmen came out over the trails to Santa Fe. Efforts were made by the Spaniards to prevent French traders from entering New Mexico and those Frenchmen who did succeed in entering Mexico were not allowed to leave, at least after the Mallet party.

The Spaniards even fomented war among the Indian nations to keep Frenchmen out, but this, too, had limited effects. French traders ascended the Arkansas and Missouri rivers and established themselves beyond the reach of Spanish officials. They bartered with the same Indians who traded with the Spaniards. Spanish policy had little effect, and the French simply ignored the fact that foreign trade was forbidden in the Spanish provinces. It is perhaps likely that, had France continued as New Mexico's eastern neighbor, the trail westward to Santa Fe would have been French. Unhappily for France, English power played its role and as a result of the French and Indian War, France lost all of Canada and the entire Mississippi Valley at one swoop. It was to be the Americans who really established that trail.

France had played a part: she was the pioneer in the westward quest for New Mexico and her beginnings were there for others to follow. French descendants would later guide the Anglo-Americans to Santa Fe. Moreover, France made the Indian conscious of the eastern merchant so that Spain could no longer exercise a monopoly. Above all, France had also shown that Spanish defenses could be breached.

When Louisiana became Spanish, an important change took place in New Mexico's status. From a frontier barrier New Mexico was changed into an integral part of New Spain's inner defense. Newly acquired Louisiana would form the outer protective wall until the beginning of the nineteenth century.

The British period, the second half of the eighteenth century, when the American Revolution occurred and technically divided the frontier of Spanish Louisiana, in fact produced some strong movements against the Spanish domains west of the Mississippi River. Both the English and Americans began a relentless pressure against the Spaniards and their possessions. It was these movements in the northern sectors that gave rise to the middle frontier of Spanish Louisiana, which in turn was the genesis of the later famous American Santa Fe Trail. This I have called the Road to Santa Fe. The movements along the Arkansas River, although also directed toward Santa Fe, and those across Louisiana and the Gulf Coast, I have called the Road to Texas. Though distinct, they form parts of the same problem, Spanish defense of its empire, and

in the earlier days of the Spanish rule in Louisiana they are hardly
separable.

II

When Spain acquired Louisiana from France, the geography of
the area northeast of New Mexico and in the area of the Upper
Missouri was unknown to the Spaniards. For example, they
believed that the Missouri had its source in the mountains north of
New Mexico. Not even the Indian inhabitants of the area were
correctly known by the Spaniards. Erroneous maps and reports
abound that prove these points.

Louisiana, strategically located, could serve as a staunch barrier
to protect wealthier Spanish lands. Military defenses were diverted
from Eastern Texas and centered around San Antonio and along
the Mississippi River. Fear of the British and the necessity for
defending its northernmost provinces in the western hemisphere
soon prompted Spain to occupy Louisiana effectively.

In view of changing patterns therefore, Spain's attitude towards
the Plains Indians also changed. Heretofore Spain had maintained
a precarious peace with whatever tribes seemed subservient and
had used those tribes to fight other tribes. But now the Jumano,
Pawnee, Kansa, Comanche and Osage could be used as an
effective barrier against the English (as they had been against the
French). This time it was hoped the effort would be better
organized and that the Indians would receive more assistance from
the Spaniards. Spain adopted French policy toward the Indians
and went to the traders-and-presents system.

In her desperate attempt to keep out British traders and
adventurers, Spain increased her Mississippi and Missouri posts in
number and strength and began policing the Mississippi River. The
principal early posts or distribution centers were Natchitoches in
the south, a post on the Arkansas in the mid-east, and St. Louis in
the northeast. In New Mexico, Santa Fe and Taos remained the
focal points. In the execution of their new policy, Spain depended
to a large extent upon officials of French heritage who had elected
to remain in the Spanish service.

Accompanying these changes was one of José de Gálvez'
(minister of Charles III) sweeping reforms, the creation of the
Commandancy General of the Provincias Internas. The northern

provinces were separated from more central Mexico, and a military government independent of viceregal authority, was established. Louisiana was attached to Havana while New Mexico remained under New Spain. Two systems evolved. Trading posts ruled in Louisiana, while New Mexico used mission and pueblo leadership and presidial guards. This eventually led to a conflict in frontier policy and later contributed to the isolation of both provinces. Under the new plan, Teodoro de Croix, *El Caballero de Croix,* became the first *comandante general,* with headquarters at Chihuahua. His program called for a well-articulated defense, which included the entire frontier and involved a rearrangement of many presidios, the establishment of a secondary defense system based on militia units in the principal pueblos, frontal attacks upon Apache warriors, and alliance with Comanche groups.

New Mexico's successive administrative proposals resulted more from the necessity of finding some remedy for Indian invasion than from the administrative challenges involved in the acquisition of Louisiana. An empty Spanish treasury prevented any real unification of northern lands. English and Indian danger from the east remained very real problems, which the formation of the Provincias Internas in no way remedied.

Spain was aware at an early date that England was a far more dangerous foe than Bourbon France had been. Louisiana was a big land and its size would act as a barrier, Spaniards reasoned. Perhaps a defensive line could be established from the Gulf of Mexico to Canada. Redon de Rassac in a memoir written in 1763, discussed the building of forts two hundred leagues above the post of Missouri and nine others among the Pani, Kansa, Cadodaqui, Opelousa, Attacapa, and others, to form a chain of forts fifty leagues apart. These were to protect the northern and eastern districts of Mexico. The plans also included ten other forts on the Mississippi.

French Governor Charles Philipe de Aubry in the early 1760s urged a strong establishment with Spanish troops to stop the English from ascending the Missouri, a proposal that excited the curiosity and cupidity of the English. International rivalry was an important matter, for Spain and France were ever fearful of British traders intruding into their territory.

And Luis Vilemont urged the Marqués de Grimaldi, Spanish secretary of state, to send an officer to the Big and Little Osage to establish a fort, as the French had done, for the English were trying to woo those tribes. Have a good *magasin*, he said, with goods for the Indians to prevent their defection to the English and the Illinois, as they had been accustomed to do in order to trade with the Canadians. Vilemont stated that the Big and Little Osage, Pani, Pani-Pique, Pataka, Ricara, La Ventane, etc., were all "savages" on the road to Santa Fe—some hostile to the Spaniards. It would have entailed little expense to the Crown to attach them to the Spaniards. Vilemont urged that a fort and troops were necessary to hold the Missouri, and another fort or depot on the Arkansas or Upper St. Francis River to take care of the other tribes.

If, however, the Spaniards were able to counter the British in the Mississippi Valley and perhaps even have a momentary edge on their rivals, the American Revolution altered the picture. Due to her inability to supply her posts and Indians, Spain completely lost economic control of the Upper Mississippi and even the Upper Missouri Valley, and failed to prevent penetration of her long frontier by British and American traders. At the end of the century, Spain made a final effort to oust British and American traders from the east bank of the Mississippi by sending spies, traders, and armed gallies up the Mississippi River. They did the same on the Missouri. But the surge of Spanish activity did not open a route to the Pacific Ocean, nor did it close the area to the British. The failure of these activities was abundantly clear to everyone when Lewis and Clark reached the Pacific via the Missouri and reported the British traders dominated the Upper Missouri and controlled the entire Indian trade of the area. In part this was due to a solely British rivalry—between the Hudson's Bay Company and the Northwest Company. Coincidental with the Lewis and Clark expedition, St. Louis traders reached Santa Fe. In this northern trade the Kiowa were to become intermediaries between Englishman and New Mexican. In 1804 a United States army officer described Spanish traders moving up the mountains to the headwaters of the Platte to trade with Americans who had gone there to meet them.

III

While officials in Spain considered Louisiana's value merely as a bulwark to protect the valuable mines in the interior of New Spain, those in Louisiana—including Carondelet, the Women of Illinois,

Governor Miró and others—had a sharper understanding of the threat posed by American and English penetration.

The French, although no longer directly involved, had suspected British intentions as early as 1776, when the Comte de Vergennes wrote the Marquis D'Ossun that Louisiana was the front wall of New Mexico, a fact which eventually might tempt the English should they ever lose their southern colonies. Fourteen years later, Philip Nolan told the governor of Louisiana that General Morgan of Virginia thought that the British would possess themselves of the Spanish settlements on the Mississippi. Nolan believe that, if war broke out, the British would descend upon Louisiana from Canada.

By 1792, Gayoso observed that from Baton Rouge to Illinois, most of the people were Anglo-Americans, and during 1793-94, it seemed probable that Spain would lose Louisiana and Florida to invading American frontiersmen aided and abetted by Republican French. Edmond Genêt's intrigues with the American Westerners projected an invasion by forces recruited in the United States, financed by France, and supported by a French fleet in the Gulf. France desired to regain Louisiana, and Westerners wanted navigation of the Mississippi, and new lands for settlement and speculation. George Rogers Clark assumed leadership of expeditions planned against St. Louis, and with that key post taken, was to descend the Mississippi to capture New Orleans, then Pensacola, and finally move on to Santa Fe. Clark knew the routes and believed the entire area to be defenseless. Even Thomas Jefferson seemed unopposed to the idea of an independent state of Louisiana. These intrigues and the current war between France and Spain alarmed the officials of Spanish Louisiana. Carondelet informed the Conde de Campo de Alange in 1794, that if the invasion from Kentucky took place all Upper Louisiana should be considered lost, with the consequences stretching as far as Santa Fe, which the enemy proposed to take. Carondelet said that St. Louis was only twenty-two-days march from Santa Fe. Fortunately for Spain, the failure of France to provide the necessary finances was largely responsible for the collapse of the various invasion plans. notably that of George Rogers Clark.

In 1797 Victor Collot observed that if the British captured Upper Louisiana, Lower Louisiana would necessarily fall, and in either English or American hands, would open the door to New Mexico. "I repeat these things, that if Upper Louisiana falls into the hands of the English or Americans, Santa Fe will be pillaged and ravaged, along with the surrounding country, because those two nations will always be in accord as long as it is a question of making money."

As can be seen, the principal reason for Spanish anxiety over Louisiana was fear that the Americans or British would penetrate Spanish western lands. Louisiana remained both the key and the barrier to New Mexico; and upon the safety of New Mexico depended the security of New Spain. The Americans coveted Louisiana for its intrinsic value. Land and farming opportunities were abundant, but along with the farmer went the trader and merchant, even greater threats to Spanish control. In August 1790, the writer of a French memoir correctly observed that "The possession of Louisiana is only useful to Spain as a barrier which protects its other establishments and guarantees them from mercantile invasion by other nations."

Spain decided on two major plans to make Louisiana an effective barrier. First, Indians and military forts would continue as bulwarks against Anglo-American encroachments, and secondly (and this was new) Spain would emphasize colonization of Louisiana lands. Immigration could provide a defense against Anglo-American attack, protect New Mexico, and through farming and industry develop Louisiana into a self-supporting unit. They first attempted to attract French Canadians, but they also offered liberal land grants and inducements to Americans, best illustrated in the Spanish Illinois country where the Americans peacefully "conquered" the area.

As for the Indian, it was the old story. As de Nava had noted in 1797, "there is too much territory to govern effectively unless the Indian is treated fairly in order to win his loyalty and prevent him from turning to the United States and England." The Indian buffer state was thus considered a necessity and, as already noted, the crucial element was presents, which meant money. The security of New Mexico depended upon Indian allegiance, and this was based on peace. As we have also seen, not all the Indians were of the same importance to Spain. The Comanche were the most powerful and numerous. Any foreign effort to win Comanche friendship was construed as a direct thrust at New Mexico, argued de Nava in 1791. Comanche importance was demonstrated by the fact that governors of New Mexico attended juntas for the purpose of selecting a new chief. If Comanche chiefs were friendly, they would bring lesser leaders into the Spanish fold. To handle the Comanche and to stop their raids, de Anza marched north from Santa Fe, through the San Luis Valley in south-central Colorado, crossed the mountains, and defeated the Comanche near Pueblo. He won the support of the Comanche and made a long-lasting peace with them, thus completing the work of Athanase de Mézières. This was a necessary forerunner to the projected overland route to St. Louis. In 1790, Governor Fernando de la Concha sent a small Spanish force with a Comanche band on an ineffectual expedition against the Pawnee. When the St. Louis officials complained, Pedro de Nava reprimanded Concha. From about 1790 permanent peace was made between the Comanche and Kiowa. In 1795 Trudeau, commandant at St. Louis, reported that Pedro Vial had gone to the Pawnee, where he remained fifteen days with some traders. He said he had come to get the Pawnee to make peace with the Comanche. He succeeded.

But fear and suspicion rather than efficient management was the usual rule in New Mexico. There was little military strength and a rather sparse population. Unhappily, too, Spain was limited by a chronically depleted treasury and by a "decadent" official class. As a result, the only viable Spanish solution to the problem of Indian control was the interpreter-scout, men of the plains used to long hardships and acquainted with Indian ways. Without their aid New Mexico would have been sorely pressed.

Typical of such men was Pedro Vial. In 1786, he marked out a direct route through the Comanche country from San Antonio to Santa Fe. The following year he journeyed from Santa Fe to Natchitoches—opening a direct route to that eastern outpost. Since the transfer of Louisiana from France to Spain, there had been no communication between Louisiana and New Mexico. During the many years that Spain had ruled these lands, Indians traversed the forgotten wastes that Frenchmen crossed, seeking New Mexican lands. In 1792 the time was ripe for some kind of an effort. Perhaps Vial undertook the initiative and persuaded Governor de la Concha that an expedition could be carried out successfully. Governor de la Concha had another motive. Louisiana was permitted to trade with the Caribbean. European merchandise imported at New Orleans, shipped to St. Louis or Natchitoches, and on by mule train to Santa Fe, would result in a forty-per-cent savings of transportation cost over that spent shipping goods from Vera Cruz to Mexico and then to Santa Fe on El Camino Real. He therefore commissioned

Vial to find the route in 1792. Yet as so often occurred, official caution took precedence over bold enterprise, and the commercial advantages of a highway from St. Louis came to exist on paper only. Vial's expedition had the double objective of opening a new route eastward and of reporting on intervening tribes. In this journey to St. Louis, Vial was aided by a friendly Indian and a French trader. He made the return journey in 1793. Vial's journey illustrated two glaring facts. The practicality of a route eastward was apparent: if Spaniards could traverse the eastern domain others would also succeed. More important, Vial's trek demonstrated a lack of Indian adhesion to Spain. The need to control New Mexican territory became more obvious. Yet Viceroy Revillagigedo's cry that what was being done in those outer eastern frontiers was very important for the defense of the interior parts of the domain of New Spain remained unheeded. Vial continued working for Spain, attempting to reconcile the Pawnee to Spanish power (1794) and possibly seeking to find out if Englishmen or Americans traded and communicated with tribes along the Spanish New Mexican frontier (1795). Orders were issued in 1795 to keep all foreigners out of New Mexico. But de Nava stated that although Americans were living at great distance from the frontier, it was not impossible that they planned to go there. Vial was to make yet another journey to St. Louis.

IV

Earlier a few Frenchmen had made their way to Santa Fe, and the French Louisiana governors Louis de Kerlérec and Pierre Vaudreuil de Cavagnat certainly had hostile designs on the territory. But after the beginning of the French and Indian War in 1754, few if any made their way to Santa Fe. There is, however, one doubtful piece of evidence that a Mr. Brevel might have gone up the Red River to Santa Fe in 1782. Dr. John Sibley, Indian agent and judge, later reported that Brevel had attempted to make a trip from San Antonio to Santa Fe but turned back because of lack of water. If Brevel had succeeded he would have been a precursor of Vial, who opened the road four years later.

During the early period of Spanish rule in Louisiana, and as a result of Spain's disparate policies in Louisiana and the Provincias

Internas concerning management of, and trade with, the Indians, Spain had to find out what was in the vast land separating Louisiana from the unknown areas acquired in 1763. In their efforts they also had to open roads and establish communications between the newly acquired lands, the Provincias Internas, and local capitals. Thus it was that Spain engaged in a remarkable series of explorations, and opened routes of communication and roads from Natchitoches to San Antonio to Santa Fe, from Santa Fe to St. Louis, from Santa Fe to California, and from Santa Fe into the Colorado area and the Great Basin. This is the period of the great work of Pedro Vial. In fact, the Spaniards spread in all directions from Santa Fe, for scattered outposts along the extended borderland called for lines of communication.

Traders engaged in trade as far north as the Gunnison River and as far west as the Colorado; Fray Silvestre Vélez de Escalante went into the Great Basin—extending the work of Don Juan María de Rivera, who entered present Utah in 1765—and attempted to find a route to California; Juan Bautista de Anza went from New Mexico to California and established overland communications; then in 1779, as governor of New Mexico, he went into southeastern Colorado. Seven years later he made an effective peace with the Comanche. Trade was conducted with the nomadic tribes of the Rocky Mountains and the plains north and east of New Mexico. Despite the fact that traders were forbidden to go beyond the frontier to the Ute country and Colorado or to the Comanche country in western Kansas, they nonetheless went. Records exist indicating that Spanish traders of New Mexico were fined for such activities in the 1780s and 1790s.

Men of daring were not lacking and Spain's frontiersmen proceeded to tie the border provinces together. De Mézières, Garcés, Vial, Escalante and de Anza, among others, displayed pathfinding energy during the last quarter of the eighteenth century scarcely less vigorous than that of the golden days of the sixteenth century. Santa Fe was the hub of long exploratory spokes thrust out in all directions to connect new outposts with old. An effort was even made to connect Louisiana with Spain's Nootka settlements on the far Northwest coast.

In 1793 Viceroy Revillagigedo warned Spanish Ministers Manuel de Godoy and Campo de Alange that war with France required precautions. In Louisiana the majority of the population was

French. Louisiana bordered the United States, and the furthest French settlement (Natchitoches) bordered Texas, which belonged to the Provincias Internas and was independent of the Spanish viceroy. In short, Louisiana was a suspect colony. Indeed there was suspicion of Jacobinism in Louisiana and also a fear of a Negro uprising. The Louisiana officials carefully watched and investigated these matters both in Lower and Upper Louisiana.

"If Louisiana was not close to Texas, which is very weak, I would not mention this now, but the present situation may expose New Spain," wrote Revillagigedo. He mentioned the possibility of an invasion, and pointed to the numerous and warlike Indians of the north. The viceroy also asked the commandant general of the Provincias Internas about the results of the recent discovery by Vial of the road from Santa Fe to Illinois, mentioning that there was a great need for further exploration of the frontier.

The projected attacks on Louisiana coincidental with Edmond Genêt's intrigues did not materialize either by land or by sea. But in October 1796, war broke out between Spain and England, and the French threat was replaced by a British threat, with fears of British attacks from Canada against Louisiana and Santa Fe. Moreover, the French were pressing Spain to retrocede Louisiana to France. These events, plus the verbal reactions of Spanish officials on the scene (the consequences of Spain having given in to the United States in signing Thomas Pinckney's Treaty of San Lorenzo in 1795), again alarmed Spain for the safety of its barrier provinces of Louisiana and New Mexico.

In 1795, the Commandant General of the Provincias Internas, Pedro de Nava, informed Godoy that although the establishments of Canada were quite distant from the frontiers of Louisiana and Texas, the English might attempt an invasion, alone or with the Americans, descending via the Lakes and the Mississippi. De Nava intended to obtain certain news from friendly Indians living on the frontiers of New Mexico and Louisiana who communicated with other tribes near American territory, and he promised troops to protect the territory under his command if Texas or New Mexico seemed in jeopardy. He advised the viceroy and others that French propaganda was entering Spanish territory, brought by colonists, and as a result of the navigation of the Mississippi having been granted to the Americans. He ordered all officials to stop the entry into Spanish territory of copies of the political book *El Desengaño del*

Hombre by Felipe Santiago Puglia (Philadelphia, 1791). He also suggested that war vessels patrol the Gulf of Mexico to the mouth of the Rio Grande and that precautions be taken against England, who had made a commercial treaty in 1794 (often called Jay's Treaty) with the Americans. The viceroy had ordered de Nava, and he in turn ordered his subordinate officers, to arrest all Frenchmen except natives of Louisiana and Mobile who were vassals of Spain, and those married to Spaniards, but to inventory their possessions.

In April 1796 Baron François Luis Hector de Carondelet, governor of Louisiana, warned Viceroy Miguel Branciforte that the Americans as well as the French were eyeing the rich mines of Mexico, which would be difficult to defend if Louisiana fell. In that same year Branciforte told Minister Manuel de Godoy that the United States was acting in bad faith, secretly trying to fool the Spaniards by allying with England. If the United States dreamt of Louisiana, he warned, England also did. Following this alliance, the conquest of Louisiana would be easy, for the English had established communication via the San Lorenzo (St. Lawrence) River, the Great Lakes, and the Mississippi from the North to the Gulf of Mexico. They could travel from Hudson's Bay and Canada, along the left of the Upper Missouri, joining the ocean at Nootka on the Pacific Northwest coast, thereby *"cubriendo el frente de nuestras Provincias Internas."* The latter provinces would have *por raiaños [rayanos] a los Americanos* who would extend their holdings along the Mississippi, and England, along the Missouri. He added, "Both those nations are ambitious, and will not limit themselves to contraband trade which they could easily undertake with the vassals of the King in the Provincias Internas and Mexico. With an increase of two regiments, and one company of cavalry, and two hundred thousand pesos extraordinary—and my preponderance over bellicose and numerous Indian nations of the South, I offer to maintain against all forces of the United States. The lack of troops and money is making us lose preponderance among Indian nations which the United States is getting through gifts and presents." Branciforte also said he was told by Carondelet that it was certain that the English had become established on the Mississippi and that they or the Americans had colonies in places near Santa Fe and on the Bay of San Bernardo on the Gulf Coast. Branciforte, however, doubted the existence of the latter colony.

In June 1796, Branciforte heard that traders from British establishments on the Missouri River had penetrated to the Platte to trade with the Pawnee, Abenaki, and other Indian nations. Other information, from Natchitoches, indicated that not far from Santa Fe the English and Americans had a post among the Yamparica Indians who lived between the sources of the Red and Arkansas rivers. Furthermore, on the Bay of San Bernardo the Americans had a settlement which, if allowed to grow, would be a source of great discomfort to the Provincias Internas and to Spain. Trader Francisco Lamothe had informed Branciforte that the Americans had a fortified blockhouse near the Yamparica, adding, "They must have crossed from Illinois, which is very possible since Pedro Vial discovered the road from Santa Fe to the Illinois last year." Lamothe offered to drive out the Americans. Carondelet also got this information from fur trader James Mackay's journal. Carondelet predicted that a prompt invasion of the Provincias Internas would indubitably follow the concession to the United States of posts that Spain held on the east bank of the Mississippi. "We cannot any longer restrain the eruption of the people of the United States west who are approaching and establishing on the east bank of the Mississippi," he wrote, continuing:

> Your Excellency must take measures in time to actively oppose the introduction of those restless people, who are a sort of determined bandits, armed with carabines, who frequently cross the Mississippi in numbers with the intention of reconnoitering, of hunting, and if they like the country, of establishing themselves in the Provincias Internas; they will arm Indians both to expand their fur trade and to make the Spaniards uneasy. Five or six thousand of those ferocious men who know neither law nor subjection are starting the American settlements and are attracting in their footsteps the prodigious emigration both from the Atlantic States and from Europe, which menaces the Provincias Internas which the Americans believe are very abundant in mines. A little bit of corn, gunpowder, and balls suffices them, a house formed from the trunk of trees serves them as shelter; their corn crop finished, they raise camp and then go further inland, always fleeing from any subordination and law [justice].

> In short, those provinces [Provincias Internas] exposed to the hostile incursions of the Americans along the Mississippi, and to those of the English along the Missouri, I consider will need for their conservation all the zeal, the activity, and the talent that Your Excellency has always manifested and to the

success of which I will be happy to contribute, if you consider
that I can contribute to the peace of these same provinces and
the kingdom which His Majesty has confided to your
vigilance.

This is only a sampling of information that Carondelet and other
frontier officials had of such activities and possible approaches to
Santa Fe.

Spain's war with England increased the problems of defending
and safeguarding Spanish possessions. The French warned Spain
in 1797 that the English were advancing toward Mexico from
Canada, from the United States, and from California. The French,
of course, wanted Spain to cede Louisiana to them, arguing that
Spain would then never have to cede anything to the United
States, and would never have anything to fear from England.
Branciforte, on October 29, 1796, reported to Spanish Minister
Godoy that Veracruz, the peninsula of California, and the
Provincias Internas were places of possible English penetration. He
summarized everything he had done to oppose the English. He
had strengthened the fortification and troops at Veracruz; increased
batteries at San Francisco, Monterey, and San Diego; erected new
Indian missions and Spanish pueblos in California; and was using
coast guard vessels. But the Provincias Internas would be in more
danger than California "whenever Anglo-Americans ally with the
English and declare war on us. They will attack Louisiana and will
drive us out as a torrent upon the Provincias Internas with the help
of [the] numerous and warlike barbarous Indians who are devoted
to them."

The long-dreaded English invasion seemed imminent in 1797.
The commandant general of the Provincias Internas wrote
Governor Fernando Chacón of New Mexico on July 14, 1797, that
the English planned an invasion with nine or ten thousand men
from Halifax. If that expedition should descend the Missouri or
some other river which entered the Mississippi, it might attack
New Mexico. He asked the governor to investigate, inquire of the
Indians, take measures, and "being sure of the authenticity of your
information, inform me promptly and I will send troops." There
was also a rumor that a Spaniard was acting as an English agent to
facilitate the expedition, and the commandant gave a description of
him. He also ordered the governor of New Mexico to send an
information-gathering expedition to the most distant Indians with

whom he had communications. In addition, there were reports of war vessels being loaded at Baltimore which, presumably via Santo Domingo, would go up the Mississippi to the Missouri or other tributaries to a point from which that very strong force could attack New Mexico.

At the same time, French General Georges H.V. Collot was making a thorough reconnaisance of the Mississippi Valley, taking notes of its value to France and the ease with which it could be conquered, suggesting plans for fortifications of St. Louis and other posts, and making maps and drawings. He uncovered what is usually called "Blount's conspiracy" (after William Blount, senator from Tennessee and coconspirator), a projected British attack on St. Louis, New Orleans, and Pensacola, aimed at taking over Spanish Florida and Louisiana. Several explanations of Collot's mission have been offered. It was suggested that the mission was to determine whether the province of Louisiana would be valuable to France, and if it might be possible to extend French commerce, either clandestinely or openly, into the Provincias Internas. Another objective of the secret Collot mission might have been to threaten Spain with invasion of the Kingdom of Mexico if she declared war on France. Collot might even have been a confidential English agent who undertook the expedition because of imminence of war between that country and Spain.

Lieutenant Colonel Carlos Howard's secret expedition in 1796 to Upper Louisiana with a squadron of Spanish war galliots was intended to offset the possibility of invasion from Canada, to drive the British from the Missouri Valley, and to protect the Mississippi frontier. Expeditions were dispatched up the Missouri and the Mississippi, spies were sent to Canada and United States, and St. Louis was fortified.

A large-scale invasion from Halifax did not materialize. Nonetheless, in 1798, with Louisiana under the governorship of Gayoso de Lemos, precautions were taken. Late in 1798, Gayoso wrote to Francisco de Saavedra, Manuel de Godoy's successor as Chief Minister, in Spain, stating that because of the importance of securing the northern frontier with Canada, Spain should demarcate a boundary from the Lake of the Woods to the Pacific, thus keeping the Colorado River well inside Spanish territory. Since both England and the United States coveted the rich fur trade of the Missouri River, Gayoso felt it essential to keep their traders out of the region. Since English traders had come from the Assiniboine along the St. Peter's River, and from the Lake of Woods to the Mandan and established themselves there, the boundary had to be defined, fortified, and defended. It was important to drive the English from the Missouri, he added, as this was the only way to prevent their penetrating the Kingdom of Mexico. In short, the security of Mexico depended upon that of Louisiana.

Pinckney's Treaty of San Lorenzo el Real in 1795 was followed by the Americans' "peaceful conquest" of the Missouri country or Spanish Illinois. American immigrants flooded the areas around Ste. Geneviève, New Madrid, and Cape Girardeau. This was encouraged in part by the Spanish policies of liberal land grants, tax exemptions and other commercial immunities, and religious tolerance; the only requirement of the immigrants was an oath of allegiance to Spain. In addition, French refugees who had been defrauded by the Scioto Company and other speculative land schemes in the American West settled in Missouri. Spain viewed this countercolonization as a means of preserving the security of her holdings. Spanish officialdom naively hoped that an oath of allegiance would miraculously transform hardy, industrious, and restless American frontiersmen into loyal Spanish subjects. More important to Americans than national allegiances were lands, farms, industries, mines, and land speculation.

The Marquis de Casa Calvo, governor of Louisiana, wrote his superior the Marquis de Someruelos, captain general at Havana, in May 1800, telling him that the Americans were not negligent. "But on the western side we are open, and the English may penetrate the interior by the upper river, as already the commercial companies of Hudson's Bay, Montreal, and Michilimackinac are doing, via the St. Peter's River, which is forty leagues above our last establishment on this river, or five hundred and forty leagues from this capital [New Orleans], as far as the [Indian] nations of the interior of New Spain."

Obviously Casa Calvo feared the British. As governor, he sent a report to Pedro de Nava, commander of the Provincias Internas, in which he stated that the English in Canada were thinking of forming an expedition, aided by various Indian nations of the Upper Mississippi, to attack "our possessions." De Nava in turn warned Governor Fernando Chacón of New Mexico. In response,

Chacón, to avert surprise if the enemy should approach the frontier, sent out one of the principal Ute captains to obtain information about the "barbarous" nations. With him, he sent three genízaros (nomadic Indians who had become incorporated into Spanish colonial society), one of whom spoke several languages, to spend the summer among the distant Indians disguised as traders. This Ute captain was to go to the Indians who were under the Spanish flag on the Missouri, for it was through that area that the English expedition would have to pass. He was to ally with Kiowa, Aas, Panana, and others. To further protect the New Mexico area from incursions, Chacón intended to send interpreters to the Comanche in the south, and to drill volunteer militiamen on Sundays.

In 1801, the government was asked to pursue a policy of granting exclusive trade concessions with the Indians on the Missouri, thus excluding foreigners from participation. Yet in 1802, Luis Vilemont, who was interested in a colonization project, and François Perrin du Lac warned the Spaniards that the Canadian companies who flouted all international law were masters of all Spanish territory from the Falls of St. Anthony to Santa Fe. Jacques D'Eglise's trading activities gave solid proof of English interference with the Indians and control of the fur trade of the Missouri. The Spaniards thus took steps to counter the English. The Missouri Company was formed for fur trading and probed up the Missouri, with James Mackay and John Evans doing heroic work for the Spaniards. Temporarily the British were ousted from among the Mandan Indians.

Nonetheless the British traders retained the upper hand. That, however, did not stop the Spaniards from trying, and try they did. Traders worked their way further up the Missouri, eventually as far as the Yellowstone River. Santa Fe became more and more crucial since it was then generally believed that the Missouri River arose in the mountains, somewhere near the city. It was natural to look upon the Missouri as the highway from St. Louis (and from Canada) to Santa Fe, and to fear that the Americans or the British might discover its headwaters. That was certainly the greatest apprehension of Carlos Delassus, lieutenant-governor of Upper Louisiana, and it was not relieved by the activites of traders out of St. Louis and Illinois during the first years of the nineteenth century. Nor were the Spaniards in the Provincias Internas relieved of these apprehensions when the Americans took over Louisiana in 1803, for the Americans were attracted to New Mexico by the same commercial motives previously held by the French.

Ignorant of the geography and of some of the Indians of the upper country, Delassus asked Régis Loisel, an experienced, knowledgeable, and intrepid hunter and trader who had spent a good deal of time in the Upper Missouri, to report to him of his knowledge. This Loisel did in 1804 and his report comprised material of utmost importance for the Spanish. It had far-reaching effects upon Spanish activities aimed at defending their new but undemarcated frontier after the United States acquisiton of Louisiana.

Reporting chiefly upon rivers that emptied in the Missouri and rose on the side of the Spanish possession or in Mexico, Loisel demonstrated how distinctly exposed were "the possessions of His Majesty to the undertakings of foreigners, who for a long time have been introducing themselves into the Upper Missouri, bribing the Indians and extracting the richest furs. They give presents to incite the Indians to peace or war, and decide the preference of their affections towards one or the other government, doing much harm to Spanish government." Loisel discovered that one could travel by water from Hudson's Bay to the mountains surrounding Santa Fe with only one portage of half a league. He noted that although the Platte River was perhaps not navigable, overland transportation between British and American trading sites, and Santa Fe, was easy, the distance slight, and the route was such that the Americans could penetrate with ease. The road could be blocked, Loisel suggested, by cultivating the Indians' favor with goods and presents. "The River Chayenne" he wrote, "also gives access to New Mexico by crossing the Black Hills [sic]. Its source is in New Mexico. Because the United States has acquired Louisiana, the undertakings of the Americans are much more to be feared, since they believe the boundaries of their purchase should be the sources of the rivers which empty into the Mississippi, although many of them take their rise in the midst of Spanish settlements. The Americans are enterprising and ambitious and will use any and all means to win the loyalty of the Indians. The Indians can be bribed, and the Americans already talk of making Mexican pesos descend the Missouri, proposing to begin contraband trade with that Kingdom. With that object in mind, the Americans are proposing to establish great merchandise magazines (depots) on the frontiers. Some men have already set out in order to prepare the way and to assure communication with Santa Fe." Loisel then offered his services to the Spanish government.

Loisel's account made a deep impression on Spanish officials in Louisiana, in the Provincias Internas, and in Mexico. The Spanish proposed to hire him after the acquisition of Louisiana by the United States, but his untimely death thwarted any further action.

What Loisel had said about men already on their way to Santa Fe proved to be correct. American officials received a steady flow of information from the Indians of Missouri and from the white hunters and traders, particularly concerning knowledge of the shortest routes to New Mexico or to Santa Fe. Traders Jeannot Metoyer and Baptiste La Lande left St. Louis in July 1804, to test such a route. Provisioned by William Morrison of Kaskaskia, they were to join Joseph Gervais, who they said was waiting for them "in the nations" and who was to guide them to Mexico. Gervais knew the road very well, having conducted Pawnee in 1803 to make peace with the governor of Santa Fe. Also in 1803, Laurent Durocher left for the same purpose; Jacques D'Eglise had left earlier in the year and since he had not returned, Lieutenant-Governor Delassus suspected that he had reached Santa Fe. Delassus remarked that St. Louis in the summer of 1804 abounded in merchandise which he knew was destined to be sent to the frontiers of Mexico: "I am of the opinion that if the greatest precautions are not taken to stop this contraband, within a short time one will see descending the Missouri, instead of furs, silver from the Mexican mines which will arrive in this post in abundance." Delassus also commented on the rumor that Lewis and Clark were similarly headed toward New Mexico and that their plan to discover the Pacific Ocean was no more than a pretext; this, however, the Spanish commandant in St. Louis doubted.

Travelers such as Etienne Véniard, Sieur de Bourgmont in 1724, the Mallet brothers in 1739, Pierre Mallet in 1751, Jean Chapuis and Louis Feuilli in 1752, and Pedro Vial in 1792 and 1793 all had shown that Santa Fe could be reached from the Missouri. That a route to Santa Fe from St. Louis not only had been discovered, but rather frequently traveled, became a certainty. It was (now), as Governor-general Manuel de Salcedo realized and wrote Spanish Minister Pedro Cevallos in 1804, most important to keep the

Americans out of the Provincias Internas, and to win the Indians of Missouri over to Spanish friendship.

But since the transfer of Louisiana to the United States had taken place and Lewis and Clark had reached the Pacific Ocean via the Missouri, the frontier of Spanish Louisiana once again shifted, with Santa Fe becoming Spanish Louisiana's new economic and commercial center. The beginnings of the Santa Fe trade would soon grow into full traffic over the Santa Fe Trail, but not until the last frontier of Spanish Louisiana had passed into history and Mexico had supplanted Spain in ownership of New Mexico. New Mexico as the perimeter bulwark province of the Spanish empire in North America, or what was left of it, girded to take countermeasures against the American intrusions, and to guard the northeastern frontier of Spanish Louisiana.

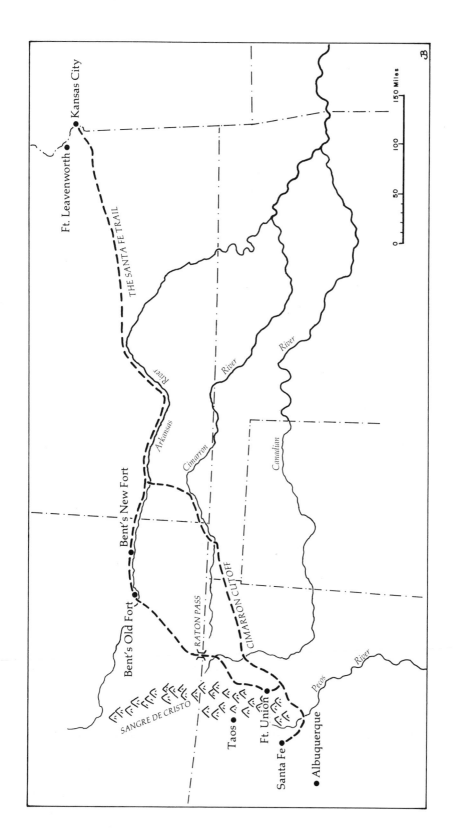

Map 5—The Santa Fe Trail

6

On the Road to Texas:
The Louisiana-Texas Frontier

In 1906, historian Isaac Joslin Cox pointed out that the Louisiana-Texas frontier was defined by many different factors. More important than physiographic features were the international struggles for expansion or self-defense, for settlement or exploitation. Louisiana had been the scene of the fruitless search for Gran Quivira; it had been claimed by La Salle for France in 1682; and Benavides and Pike had dreamt of opening the unexplored area. It was also the scene of individual occupations by explorer, missionary, conquistador, trader, and Indian agent. When it eventually became a Spanish colony in 1762, the rivalry, in all its forms, that Louisiana had experienced during the French period, continued. Under the Spaniards, Louisiana was within the jurisdiction of Cuba, while New Mexico, whose Spanish forces kept back the French, was a part of New Spain. After 1776 Louisiana frequently became independent from Mexico in action.

The boundaries of Louisiana had never been solidly and definitively determined. The line of practical effectiveness was considered to be between Natchitoches and Los Adaes, at the Arroyo Hondo east of the Sabine River. This was officially the case at least when Louisiana was under French rule and while Texas was under Spanish jurisdiction. The vagueness of the boundary lines was to have a tremendous effect upon the frontier of Spanish Louisiana. The northern boundaries were not only unsettled and undefined, but, in fact, were unknown and unexplored. When the United States purchased it, she reaped advantages from that muddled state of boundary affairs.

There had been little thought given to the boundary question, and less action taken, before 1804. About 1760, a proposed line marked the spheres of influence among the Indians, keeping separate French-influenced Indians from Spanish-influenced Apache. Fray Agustín Morfí mentioned in his *Memorias* (ca. 1781) that the boundary lay between Los Adaes and Natchitoches, while Spanish governor Esteban Miró urged the adoption of the Sabine River (shown as a boundary in Langaras' map of 1799) as the boundary.

Territorial expansion from New Mexico was limited, although Spain claimed lands as far away as the Pacific to the west, and to Arkansas and Mississippi on the north and east. The grandiose claims of the Spaniards greatly diminished with the passage of time as the result of both Spanish administrative divisions and foreign encroachments. Effectively, New Mexico did not expand much beyond the region of original colonization in the Rio Grande Valley. It was separated from the Plains by the Sangre de Cristo and other ranges of the Rocky Mountain chain.

Together with Texas, New Mexico served as a protective buffer for Spain's more valuable land to the south. Until 1776, it was under the control of a governor, often ad-interim, at Santa Fe. After that date, the governor was responsible to the commandant general of the Provincias Internas (at Chihuahua and Durango), an official who remained virtually independent of the viceroy but who was responsible to the King. New Mexico was never adequately garrisoned or supplied. It was generally protected only by citizen militias, poorly organized and ill-equipped forces drawn from the Spanish and Indian inhabitants. New Mexico suffered depredations from Apache, Navajo, Comanche, and Ute (although by 1786 de Anza had pacified the powerful Comanche), as well as faced disturbing threats from foreigners.

Texas, also part of the Provincias Internas, had borne the brunt of Franco-Spanish rivalry during the first part of the eighteenth century. From Natchitoches and the Nassonite post among the Cadodacho, French traders went among the Indians of Texas as far as the Lower Trinity River. The French wanted to penetrate New Mexico from these posts, but were confronted by three major obstacles: the protective jealousy of Spain; the Apache who blocked the Red River route; and the hostility of the Comanche along the Missouri and Arkansas rivers. Eventually the French succeeded in breaking through the Comanche barrier, and subsequently increased their aggressive actions along the Texas border. In 1753

Louis de Kerlérec, then governor of French Louisiana, proposed that the French break through the Apache barrier to open trade with the interior of Mexico. The Spaniards between Louisiana and Texas, as well as the governor of New Mexico, were ordered to stop French trafficking with the Indians of Texas. The establishment in 1756 of the small presidio of San Agustín de Ahumada on the Trinity curbed the activities of traders temporarily, but by 1759 French trading was reported at the mouth of the Brazos, and French traders and goods continued to enter Spanish Texas. For some time the Indians living in that part of Texas between the plains culture of the Comanche and the agrarian East Texas tribes served as middlemen in trade, sending horses stolen by the Comanche from Spaniards and Indians to the east, and guns and farm products west to the Plains warriors. Spain's policy to win the allegiance of all the tribes, at least for a time, was stymied.

At its largest the Louisiana-Texas frontier zone extended between the Lower Mississippi and Rio Grande valleys and between the Gulf of Mexico and the Rocky Mountains; although the geography of that great extent of territory was not then accurately known, it was thought that the Red River led to Mexico, that the Platte River rose in the mountains of New Mexico, and obviously that the Gulf Coast ran all along the extent of this frontier on the Gulf of Mexico side. This frontier had come into being when La Salle established his colony in Texas in order to elicit trade in time of peace and acquire the rich Mexican silver mines (in the event of war.)

II

By the Treaty of Fontainebleau in 1762, the French King gave to his Spanish cousin all of Louisiana west of the Mississippi. The entire Franco-Spanish, Louisiana-Texas frontier was obliterated, the old frontier technically wiped out and jumped from Texas to the Mississippi River, where the Spaniards faced their new neighbors, the English. The excitable French neighbors were replaced by the implacably grasping, and more feared, Englishmen. The aggressive English settlers, after having founded settlements on the Atlantic coast, had long since been drifting over the mountains into the fertile valleys of the Mississippi and its tributaries, and some had penetrated French Louisiana and into Spanish territory as well. Previously, Spanish officials had found some sense of security in the fact that the French outposts along the Mississippi acted as a buffer to Spanish dominion. Quite early, as governor-general of Spanish Louisiana, Luis de Unzaga y Amezaga had seen the English as a menace to Spain west of the Mississippi. Later, when the American Revolutionary war broke out, Unzaga was alarmed by the lack of sufficient Spanish troops, forts, and skilled or efficient militia to defend and stop the enemy from immigrating into and settling Spanish territory.

And, indeed, since the very beginning of their takeover of gigantic Louisiana, there was abundant evidence that Spanish fears were well-founded. For nearly half a century Spain had been unable to keep Texas free of French trading and tampering with the Indians, and she continued to be in the same position vis-à-vis the English. Moreover, Texas, formerly an outer province and buffer, was now an interior province. There was no longer need for military establishments in Eastern Texas since Spanish jurisdiction had with one stroke been extended to the Mississippi. Louisiana as a Spanish colony had special commercial privileges not granted to other Spanish provinces in New Spain and Texas. Therefore, in a sense, the Louisiana-Texas border was reemphasized.

The acquisition of Louisiana and the end of the Seven Years War prompted the new young King of Spain, Charles III, to reassess both his empire and his policies. One of the outstanding administrative reforms dating from Charles' reign was José de Gálvez' creation in 1776 of the Comandancia General de Provincias Internas. This provided for the defense of the large and extensive northern frontier of New Spain, including the northern states of modern Mexico and the newly acquired California. It became, in effect, an agency of government practically independent from the viceroyalty in far away Mexico City. Under its first commandant, Teodoro de Croix, plans for defense and for Indian control were drafted. Louisiana, however, was not included in the Provincias Internas and did not figure prominently in the new strategies. At that time the Lipan Apache were the big problem, probably as a result of the relentless Comanche pressure which had forced the Apache southward where they were harassing Texas settlements. New Mexico was naturally more concerned with the Indian problem than with the distant British. Croix's plans for war against the Apache never materialized because of the imminent war with England. The Marquis de Rubí who had made an inspection trip of the Interior Provinces a decade earlier had recommended building fifteen frontier defense posts, forty leagues apart reaching from Bahía del Espíritu Santo near the mouth of the San Antonio River, to the head of the Gulf of California. This meant abandoning East Texas. De Mézières offered a different plan for defense which called for the erection of presidios among the Nations of the North in Texas in order to war against hostile Indians, especially the Apache. He suggested recruiting the French in Louisiana, as soldiers. His purpose was to present a serious obstacle to the threatened advance of the English. He pointed out to the Baron de Riperdá, July 4, 1772, the danger of the English settled on the Mississippi River, the new boundary between Spanish and British Louisiana. The tributaries of that river from the west provided easy English access to Texas and New Mexico. "Notorious," therefore, "is the opportunity which the English (whose dexterity and skill in making use of rivers are patent) have to come down by water at any time with the security afforded by vast and unpopulated lands, and with little or no opposition. [They could] bring the supplies they wish to invade our provinces, unless the most prompt and effective remedy is provided to anticipate them." De Mézières suggested as a remedy the establishment of a presidio or fort where requested by Indians. Presidios, offers of peace, and the settling of the Comanche would result in a cordon which would extend to the mountains of New Mexico and keep the English out. Furthermore, he pointed out that the Osage were already hostile and presented a threat, and that the English were giving the Indians of Texas arms to incite them against the Spanish. Also, the English were alienating the Pawnee, and, through them, influencing the Taovaya. De Mézières wanted a line of presidios reaching from the Mississippi River to New Mexico. He also suggested the establishment of trade along the Trinity River as a means of gaining the good will of the Indians.

Rubí's and de Mézières' suggestions were debated for years but neither was implemented. East Texas was abandoned and the post of Bucareli was established on the Trinity, partly to break up illicit trade with the English. But illicit trade was never effectively stopped.

Gil y Barbo (Ybarbo), colonizer at the Trinity River post, also searched for—and found—some Englishmen up the Sabine and

Neches rivers, and mapped the coast from the Sabine to the Trinity. But opposition from Texas settlers forced the abandonment of Bucareli. Nacogdoches, replacing Los Adaes, was looked upon to maintain Spanish influence among the Indians, and act as a makeweight against the Anglo-Americans.

Spain feared inroads from the English all up and down the Mississippi. She strenghtened her posts at St. Louis and slightly increased her influence in present Iowa. Spanish Texas, however, feared hostility from the Red River tribes, citing English influence among them. By 1772 English firearms and goods had already appeared in the Taovaya country. It was urged that Texas move its defense line to the Taovaya country on the Red, to which point the Panimaha Indians, disturbed by the cession of Lousiana, were moving from the Missouri. The proposition was discussed, but never approved.

Spain needed a new Indian policy suited to their newly acquired, formerly French, Louisiana. The Spaniards now had to win the allegiance of those Indians who, under the French, had been their former enemies. Moreover, all tribes from the mouth of the Sabine to Canada had to be kept hostile to the advancing English: friendly tribes were urged to pillage English traders. The Spaniards were also fearful that the Anglo-Americans would tamper with the southwestern tribes and invade Spanish territory. Hence, Spain's new Indain policy included the adoption of French methods of trading and former French officials were persuaded to enter into the Spanish setup.

Yet, the officials of Louisiana and Texas did not see eye to eye, and worked at cross purposes in adopting and enforcing regulations of the new Indian policy. Louisiana officials continued previous policy, while Texas officials followed contradictory Indian policies as set down by their superiors in far away Mexico. Jurisdictional disputes resulted. By law New Spain prohibited Nachitoches traders from buying horses and mules from the Taovaya, and hence that tribe sold them, as before, to contraband traders of Arkansas and to Indian tribes of Missouri. Natchitoches, which needed horses, was deprived both of their use, and of the profits of trading in them. This naturally encouraged horse stealing in Spanish settlements. The Natchitoches traders wanted the restrictions removed so they could compete with the contrabandists of Arkansas. Another aspect of the question of jurisdiction arose with regard to gift giving to the Nations of the North. Those nations had been getting their presents including firearms, from Natchitoches. Texas, however, prohibited the sale of firearms to the Indians.

Among the tribes of the Louisiana-Texas frontier, hostilities engendered by previous French and Spanish rivalry had not entirely subsided, and de Mézières was assigned the task of reconciling the Indians with the new Spanish administration. He made numerous journeys into the Indian country, negotiated treaties, and evicted unauthorized traders replacing them with those properly licensed. Maintenance of peace, essential to the safety of the settlements, was rendered even more difficult by the intrusions of English traders from West Florida (especially from Natchez) and from Illinois. To complicate things further English merchants along the Mississippi also kept unlicensed French traders in Louisiana supplied with goods.

The English entered Spanish territory on the southwestern border either by way of the coast, or across Louisiana to various parts of the Texas frontier. Tribes as far west as the Texas border were contacting the English by 1768 to obtain goods; in 1769, four Englishmen were found to be living at or near Natchitoches; and by 1772, an English party went eastward to Natchitoches with cattle and other materials bought at San Antonio. In that same year the use of English firearms by the Taovaya on the Upper Red River was discovered, and several English merchants at Opelousas boasted that they would trade any place they pleased. Before 1772 several shipwrecked English mariners had been found on the Texas coast, and in October 1773, English traders were reported crossing Louisiana. This prompted an order from the governor of Louisiana to de Mézières to stop them.

De Mézières, lieutenant-governor at Natchitoches, did his best service by winning the allegiance of the Nations of the North for Spain, and by maintaining this allegiance in both Louisiana and Texas. In 1774, it was reported that an Englishman identified as Juan Hamilton and others continued to make journeys to the mouth of the Trinity by buy stolen horses and mules from the Indians. Jerome Matalinche, reported to be the agent of the English merchants from Fort Manchac was trading on the Neches. In 1777, the town of Bucareli on the Trinity reported that an English vessel was stranded at the mouth of the Neches. Gil y Barbo found the boat, as well as an Englishman from it. Said Englishman had apparently been stranded long enough to plant a crop there.

During 1772-73, the Panimaha Indians, moving south from the Missouri country were securing English goods and guns for the Taovaya. In return, they received horses. But it wasn't until 1778 that de Mézières reported that English traders had appeared, beginning in the previous fall, among the Taovaya. In the same year, Teodoro de Croix, commandant general of the Interior Provinces, said that he was opposed to the sale of arms to the Indian Nations of the North. But he admitted that if that policy were enforced, the Spaniards would lose their Indian allies to the English, "who miss no chance to introduce themselves among the Indians, both for the profit gained from barter, and for the welcome and gratitude with which the Indians receive them."

Unlicensed trade was never entirely suppressed, largely on account of these jurisdictional disputes and because of divergent interests on the parts of traders and government officials. Activities of traders on the Texas border continued to be a source of friction between Texas and Louisiana.

In 1783, Domingo Cabello, who succeeded Riperdá as governor of Texas, complained to Miró that Louisiana traders were supplying arms to Texas tribes, who in turn traded them over to hostile Lipan Apache. Miró attempted, unsuccessfully, to prohibit trade to Texas. Within Louisiana, Natchitoches officials objected to Ouachita traders among the Caddo. And both Louisiana and Texas officials complained of the trade, originating in Spanish Illinois, with the Osage (who were pushing south and attacking Indians in the Arkansas and Red river valleys). The officials of the Provincias Internas and the Mexican viceroy also objected to trade carried on by French inhabitants of Louisiana. There the Bidai (or Vidai) and Attakapa Indians served as intermediaries between the French in Louisiana and the Apache in Texas. Trading for horses and cattle stolen in Texas the French kept the Apache supplied with guns. The need to strengthen Spain's weak hold on her far flung northern frontier against the impact of the American pioneer became a major administrative concern.

III

South of Illinois Country and the key center of St. Louis, the Spanish also faced the danger of English infiltration. English traders had penetrated the Arkansas Valley, where they were never completely checked. They represented an ever present threat to the Spanish in Arkansas who feared that the English might penetrate from there to Mexico. To consolidate their position, the English formed a small establishment between the White and Arkansas rivers and plied the Indians with brandy. The Arkansas Indians soon realized that the English would supply them with goods and presents when those from the Spaniards were not satisfactory. The Chi Indians, in fact incited by the English, fought the Quapaw, whom the English had had difficulty in winning over. On January 13, 1769, Alejandro de Clouet noted that the Chi, led by two Englishmen, and a Canadian named Charpentier, pillaged for the second time "our" French hunters on the Arkansas River. In 1777, a refuge for river pirates and English vagabonds was founded at El Cadrón (near present-day Little Rock).

The Arkansas Post, at the mouth of that river, center of Spanish control over Indians in the region, was undermined when the English built a store on the bluff directly opposite. The store soon became a canteen for the Indians. These Indians, left to their own devices, were not difficult to deal with. The Spanish Arkansas Post commander, however, whose duty was to keep out the English and to encourage Arkansas hostility toward them, was disturbed by the presence of a "loose" English woman settled across the river who dispensed liquor to the Indians. It appeared certain to Alejandro de Clouet that her role would become only that of a harlot for the red men. In fact, she actively sought to persuade the Indians to expel de Clouet and become dependent on the English.

The Osage from the north, the Chickasaw from the south, and the Comanche and Apache from the west further complicated things. The Chickasaw, as tools of the English, were constantly incited to make war on the Arkansas. The Osage, on the other hand, needed no one to convince them to make war against the Arkansas—war was their natural state—and they especially made trouble for hunters and traders along the Arkansas River. In addition, the English colonists, disgusted by the Proclamation of 1763 which barred them from trading west to, and beyond, the Mississippi, became disruptive.

In the years immediately preceding the American Revolution, the contest for the commercial control of Louisiana was growing more and more intense, with the odds in favor of the British. Both Spain and England knew that this trade was a vital factor in the

development of the West. Under the governorship of Bernardo de
Gálvez, the British found themselves rather suddenly treated with
great suspicion and finally excluded altogether.

Balthazar de Villiers, Spanish commandant at Arkansas Post, on
June 11, 1778, urged Governor Gálvez to construct a fort on the
banks of the Arkansas: "An establishment on this river seems of
great importance both to protect our hunters (who, if they are not
disturbed by the Osage and the Taovaya, pour into the province
large amounts of tallow, fresh oil, and furs of all sorts) and to be
on guard against the enterprises of the English who, in time of
war, might penetrate as far as the frontiers of New Mexico." And
in the same letter: "Everyone knows that these savages will belong
to those who give them the most; that not receiving anything, or
practically nothing from Spain, they will go to the English in an
instant, which makes one realize the necessity of forming a
respectable establishment on this river." England in her period
alongside Spanish lands had penetrated Louisiana from the north
and from the east. In this area English trade had become profitable
and experienced men had been left in the country to guide others
into Spanish lands.

During the Revolution, Commandant de Villiers was very
concerned about the influence of English traders with the Arkansas
Indians, and he was warned by Governor Gálvez not to allow any
English on the frontier. The Spanish commandant subsequently
crossed the Mississippi River on November 22, 1780, took formal
possession of the east bank in the name of the King of Spain.
During the latter part of the Revolution, a band of Chickasaw
under the leadership of British Captain James Colbert, interrupted
navigation along the Mississippi. One of his captives was Madame
Cruzat, wife of Francisco Cruzat, Spanish lieutenant-governor of
Illinois. She later informed New Orleans of Colbert's plan to attack
Arkansas Post. In 1783 Colbert did unsuccessfully attack and lay
siege to Arkansas Post which was stoutly defended by
Commandant Jacobo Dubreuil. Dubreuil also told Gálvez that the
Arkansas Post was instrumental in preventing eventual penetration
of the kingdom of Mexico. But in August 1783, a party of
Chickasaw came to make peace with the Spaniards.

By 1782 American settlers were firmly established in the
Mississippi Valley, as a result of the inexorable westward march of
the Anglo-American frontiersmen. With the restraining hand of

British control removed, the Spaniards were now face to face with the first independent power in the New World, a power consumed by the desire to expand. Even the Indians begged Spanish Commandant Dubreuil not to permit the English and the Americans to settle along the central Mississippi. Spain's frontier difficulties had in reality only started.

The Spanish policies after 1783, aimed at preventing incursions into Spanish territory, were criticized by Spanish commandants at Arkansas, St. Louis, and elsewhere. Higher officials recommended building more forts, patrolling the Mississippi with gunboats, befriending Indians, and occasionally inviting Americans to settle on Spanish lands. Colonists not only feared the aggressive American, but resented the idea that Louisiana's only value to Spain was that of a bulwark, an advance area designed to protect the more valuable mines in the interior and to fortify the frontier of New Spain. This resentment was expressed by many Spaniards—by "The Women of Illinois" in 1790; by Spanish Governor Esteban Miró in 1792. The policies were viewed as a corollary to the strategy of creating an Indian buffer state tied to Spain by alliances, trade, and military posts. To reach Santa Fe the traveler had to cross Indian territory between the Mississippi and that city. The problem became that of keeping the Indians friendly, and loyal to Spain. Thus alliance, fort, trader, and gifts to Indians became synonymous with Spain's Indian relations. The crux was gifts—for without them Indians rarely cooperated; and gifts required money. However, both money and manpower to enact the policies were not forthcoming. Since there were others who would give presents to the Indians, it is not surprising that in 1796, Luis de Blanc, commandant at Natchitoches, could express the same anxiety over American aggression that the Spanish had felt for over a hundred years toward the French and English.

Carondelet later correctly sized up the situation of the Arkansas country: Its importance stemmed not only from the fact that it contained two major waterways—the Arkansas and Canadian rivers leading to Santa Fe and Taos, and the Red River leading into the Spanish Southwest—but it also encompassed an established overland route to Lower Louisiana, connecting the Arkansas Post with Natchitoches. (From earliest times a contraband trade in horses and mules had grown up between the Indians, the Arkansas and those people living along the south part of the land route.) Thus, in Arkansas country two entry roads, one to Texas, and one to New Mexico, originated.

Spain, after taking Louisiana, continued French efforts to reenforce communication between the widely separated centers of St. Louis, the Arkansas Post, San Antonio, and Santa Fe. French traders had learned, after much difficulty, how to conciliate the Comanche and the Apache, and French officials such as de Clouet, de Villiers, and de Mézières had used their influence in transferring this affection for the French traders to the Spaniards. The foundations were laid for subsequent successful Spanish efforts. English traders and contrabandists south of Arkansas, in the Red River Valley were probably more active. They had infiltrated quickly to Natchitoches and beyond, and were a very great source of worry to the Spaniards. As early as 1768, Ulloa had warned Governor O'Conor of Texas that the Yatasí Indians would go to the English frontier to get what they wanted, and de Mézières warned that tribes along the Louisiana-Texas border were buying goods from Englishmen. Two years later Spanish-licensed traders were instructed that no English merchants or merchandise were to enter Spanish territory. Riperdá reported to the viceroy that in spite of the exlusion policy, Indians continued to receive better and cheaper goods from the English. He proposed a line of presidios from the Mississippi to New Mexico.

In 1772 José de Areche warned that Indians were stealing horses and using them to obtain goods from the English. He reaffirmed the necessity of keeping Indians loyal to Spain so that they might act as a bulwark against the English in times of war. De Mézières advised Riperdá that the Panimaha were advertising among the Indians the advantages of trade with the English; that it was easy for the English to penetrate to Texas and New Mexico; and that it was absolutely necessary to construct a cordon of settlements, to extend to the New Mexican mountains, in order to keep out the English. He mentioned that the English had been navigating the Missouri River for a long time, and reported (July 16, 1772) that the English were trading with the Yscani, Tuacana, and Taovaya. Riperdá passed this information on to the viceroy.

Julio Arriaga, general minister of the Indies, wrote Unzaga from Aránjuez, Spain, on May 30, 1774, that the English traders' intrusions among the Indians must be stopped; the King then ordered de Mézières to oust the English. De Mézières wrote

Unzaga that the English were journeying to the mouth of the Trinity River to buy horses and mules from the Indians (1774). In 1777 he advised Gálvez of the existence of a band of Englishmen with merchandise at El Cadrón on the Arkansas; and on February 20, 1778, he wrote the viceroy that the Spaniards should explore the Missouri especially since the English were thinking of doing the same. In 1778 de Mézières told Croix that the Taovaya had asked for Spanish traders. If that request were met it would enable the Spaniards to deal with friendly nations in the north, and contribute to the winning over of the Comanche and Osage. The Spaniards would then be able to secure information about remote tribes; prevent any new English invasion; and establish easy access to, and communication with, Natchitoches, Illinois, New Mexico, and San Antonio. He also said that two Englishmen had come via the Arkansas River to establish trade and friendship with the Taovaya, but that the Indians had rejected them. Finally, Croix wrote to José de Gálvez in Spain, delineating de Mézières' suggestions.

Others also wrote Gálvez with similar news and suggestions. Gil y Barbo told of the English on the Gulf coast, who had stayed long enough to grow a crop. De Villiers at Arkansas Post urged Gálvez to build a fort on the banks of the Arkansas to protect hunters and guard against the English. By 1778, De Mézières told Croix that he feared he would be defeated by the aggressive English if measures were not taken.

The American Revolutionary War did not seriously affect the inroads of the English traders into Spanish territory, nor did it allay the fears of the Spanish. The treaty substituting the United States for England as the owner of the east bank of the Mississippi made little difference to the Spaniards. But once the fighting was over and the United States independent, Spain was forced to take cognizance of the American frontiersman's inherent disregard for higher authority and his propensity for finding out what lay beyond the next mountain or river. Warnings about Americans were forthcoming. Juan Gasiot, a French agent among the Indians, warned Felipe de Neve, commandant of the Provincias Internas, of the serious danger to Spain from the newly independent United States. Gasiot predicted that the Americans would make frequent incursions to establish trade with the natives, and that when they eventually reached Spanish borders they would be implacable. He recommended strong and immediate steps to win the support of the Indians, establishment of better communications between the scattered frontier provinces, and other defensive measures. Texas took on greater importance, as did Nacogdoches, as the English and Americans began to make deeper inroads into the area. Unfortunately, the Spanish government was opposed to free trade between Louisiana and Texas, was against establishing posts on the Gulf, and refused to adopt the Sabine as the boundary between Louisiana and Texas.

That there were many incursions into Texas is shown by a few later facts. As has been mentioned, the first French arrived in that area in 1778, the first Englishman in 1783, the first Irishman in 1786, and the first American in 1789. In 1804 there were sixty-eight foreigners living there, fifty of whom had been there for over three years; among these were between thirteen and twenty Americans. These were more than transient traders. All this occurred despite the exclusion policy of Spain. The need for communication routes was imperative, and Pedro Vial performed magnificent service in opening up such routes. These included one from the southeast, from Bexar to Santa Fe and one from Santa Fe to St. Louis. This last had been suggested by Fernando de la Concha to Jacobo Loyola de Ugarte as early as 1789, as part of the effort to open a new and cheaper route by which European goods could reach New Mexico. Much later this became the Santa Fe Trail. But in 1792, as often happens, official caution took precedence over bold enterprise, and the commercial advantages of a highway from St. Louis to Santa Fe came to exist on paper only. Ugarte had also been interested in a system of roads that would bind more closely the several frontier provinces; he envisioned linking Texas, New Mexico, and Louisiana with Sonora and California to promote exchange of information, reciprocity of military assistance, and development of common interests. He supervised the discovery of several routes that were feasible for commerce, although no prosperous trade resulted immediately, and he did provide some of the explorer-pathfinders with instructions.

With communications and routes established between Santa Fe, St. Louis, Natchitoches and San Antonio, the new Indian policy was to appease the Indians at all costs, and to establish defense points and fortifications. Juan de Ugalde, commandant general of the Provincias Internas, recommended improving the fortifications of La Bahía and Nacogdoches, which was imperative since the latter was the gateway to Texas for intruding traders, travelers, and contrabandists. Both the commandants of the Provincias Internas and Texas issued strong orders against illicit trade with Louisiana, and the admission of foreigners, but the Louisiana officials were powerless. Louis de Blanc, commandant at Natchitoches, admitted openly that he could not prevent the Americans from penetrating Texas. In 1792 he told Carondelet that foreigners were constantly coming to Natchitoches to trade, and that merchants were scattered throughout his district. The Texas Indians had been supplied from this Spanish post until the death of de Mézières, but the new purveyor appointed by the commandant general of the Provincias Internas did not have sufficient capital to supply the Indians. De Blanc also told Carondelet that Anglo-Americans were beginning to present themselves in his post with passports from commandants of the different posts of Louisiana—"a thing that is not at all desirable." De Blanc feared "the evil conduct of those depraved people whom we have just cause to suspect, and ought to prevent from introducing themselves into the provinces of New Spain." Miró also pointed out the danger and ordered intrusions of Americans stopped. Cruzat and Pérez complained continually about English and American traders infiltrating. Commandants at St. Louis warned of American and English "vagabonds" who intended to go into the province of New Mexico.

This problem was ubiquitous in all parts of Spanish Louisiana. Americans were in Texas, and the Captain General of Havana, Luis de Las Casas, warned Carondelet about it, he having been forewarned by the viceroy of Mexico. The viceroy (using information from his frontier officials) spoke of the injuries to Texas caused by the activities of traders from the United States; he hoped that Carondelet would take most rigid measures to repress it, urging him to act in accord with the governor of Texas. The viceroy's information dated July 31, 1792, had come from the commandant at Bahía del Espíritu Santo. It stated that the Apache were getting arms and ammunition through the Attakapa Indians, via the posts of Attakapas and Opelousas. The outbreak of the French Revolution and the resultant war against France increased the worries of the Spaniards for the safety of Louisiana, both for its own sake and for its function as protective buffer for New Mexico and Texas. There were rumors to the effect that England might have emissaries among the tribes of East Texas who were to subvert the Indians' loyalty. Spain sent out reconnaissance expeditions to investigate. Warnings about the possible loss of Louisiana and impending invasion of the Provincias Internas were based largely on the knowledge of French, English, and American intrigues. Genêt's intrigues, as planned by George Rogers Clark, called for invasion and threw fear into the hearts of all Spanish officials. The documentation concerning these affairs is far too extensive to recount here. After England and Spain went to war in 1796, the Spanish viceroy, more than ever, feared an alliance of England and the United States for the purpose of invading the Provincias Internas. He considered the Provincias Internas a greater risk than California, and believed that the Anglo-Americans would pounce upon them, driving out the Spaniards with the aid and help of the numerous and warlike Indians. He had heard that the Americans had a settlement in the Bay of San Bernardo and built a blockhouse near the Yamparica. In fact, even Carondelet predicted the invasion of the Provincias Internas after, in the Treaty of 1795, Spain granted the Americans the right of navigation on the Mississippi and gave up the Spanish settlements on the east bank above the thirty-first parallel. That treaty left the border along the Mississippi unprotected. Carondelet wrote, "We cannot any longer restrain the eruption of the people from the United States West who are approaching and establishing on the east bank of the Mississippi." Suspicion and fear of invasion were the talk of Spanish officials high and low. William Blount's conspiracy proposing attacks on Spanish possessions, as divulged by the French general Collot, added to their fears. Even that great intriguer, James Wilkinson, used the fear of a British invasion of Spanish territory to his own advantage in order to get commercial concessions out of the Spaniards. Carlos Martínez de Yrujo in Philadelphia spent his time warning Spanish officials in Havana, New Orleans, Mexico, and on the frontier, as well as in Spain, of impending British invasions. This seemed all the more plausible since England and Spain were at war. Pedro de Nava suggested transforming New Orleans into a second Gibraltar and erecting equally strong defenses and fortifications at St. Louis, the key entry and defense points for Louisiana. The year 1797 was one of crisis.

In 1797, de Nava, as commandant general of the Provincias Internas, informed Spain directly that during the previous year the Choctaw of Natchitoches had interrupted the quietude of Texas.

The Choctaw later petitioned to be allowed to move to Texas, but were refused. Carondelet ordered the commandants to watch, and prevent arms going into Texas; but in Louisiana there continued open trade in arms for furs, and liquor was widely used among the Indians. Carondelet said that the English had ambitions to extend their trading activities, via the Missouri, and that Americans intended to do likewise. The Caddo were being offered goods cheaper by the English, and would aid the Choctaw against their enemies. In short, Carondelet urged vigilance. At the same time, de Nava also sent documents showing that England and the Anglo-Americans were preparing to conduct hostilities against the Province of Louisiana. The Americans were making movements to take possession of Natchez, the English to descend the Mississippi and attack St. Louis.

But Anglo-Americans had been pushing their way across the Mississippi ever since 1763. From the time the British had occupied West Florida, Anglo-Americans from the coast had gone to the Yazoo and Natchez. West Florida had become a good base for the English to trade with Louisiana. The Anglo-Americans approached Spanish territory in Illinois, in West Florida, and in Lower Louisiana. They advanced up the Red and Ouachita rivers as far as the Texas-Louisiana frontier, with Indian traders and horse drovers leading the way. There were many Americans in Natchez. Even the Spaniards in Natchez opened and kept up intercourse with Texas through Natchitoches and made commercial possibilities known to Americans. But there were also immigrants who were invited to settle in Spanish Louisiana with the hope that they would form a barrier to the onrush of the reckless American frontiersmen. Luis Vilemont proposed the idea that populating Louisiana was the only way to maintain it as a buffer and barrier to aggressive Americans on the road to Texas and New Mexico. Refugees from the former French colony Acadia had been invited to settle the area. Large colonization grants to the Marquis de Maison Rouge and to the Baron de Bastrop were prompted by the same idea. By 1798-99, the number of American settlers in West Louisiana and even in Texas was increasing. Colonies were planned along the Calcasieu River in Louisiana; and Benjamin Fooy's Dutchmen settled at Esperanza in Arkansas; and Arkansas itself, which never was attractive to Americans, received some settlers.

The American advance towards Texas had been preceded by settlers and Americans in the Red and Ouachita river valleys. Once again Indian traders and horse drovers paved the way for farmers and settlers, who followed closely behind. An American was granted land on the Arroyo Hondo in 1791. Avoyelles became the natural meeting place for the traders and travelers going by water to and from Natchitoches, Rapides, and New Orleans. Emigrés were encouraged to settle and given land grants and concessions, as in the cases of Maison Rouge, Baron de Bastrop, and others. Spain not only granted land for these settlers, but even agreed to aid in settlement. Instead of Catholics, however, they got many Protestants, especially among Americans. These American frontiersmen did not respect boundaries, or authority, laws or decrees. Most of them were under the jurisdiction of Louisiana, although the area between the Marmento and Sabine rivers was disputed. The Texas policy of exclusion proved to be more and more difficult to maintain, and as a barrier to Americans, was indeed feeble. Before 1800 the advance guard of American settlers had crossed the Sabine, opening the way into Texas. Lower Louisiana had also been crossed and settlers had penetrated well into Texas.

The Mississippi Valley had attracted the Americans by the prospect of good agricultural land. Texas offered inducements of excellent grazing country, suited for large stock ranches, and large land grants. Texas, too, was a veritable horse trader's paradise; horse raising and horse trading became dominant during the American occupation of Texas. A further inducement was the Indian trade.

Ten Louisianians, among whom were English traders, reached the Taovaya and Comanche with guns. These Indians defended the intruders against a Spanish punitive expedition. In 1797, the Tawakoni, Tankawa, and Kichai Indians got arms from the Huase to whom they gave horses and cattle. The Huase, in turn, traded horses and cattle to the Anglo-Americans for prohibited arms, powder, and lead. Americans went to Texas in defiance of all prohibiting regulations: Spain excluded Frenchmen. But the contraband trade between Louisiana and Texas increased, and many followed that profession, among whom Philp Nolan was the best known.

The exploits of Philip Nolan increased Spanish suspicions about the designs of the Anglo-Americans, as did the purchase of Louisiana. But once again clashes of policy intruded. Juan José Elguezábal, ad-interim governor of Texas, desired and approved petitions of foreigners to settle in Spanish Texas, while his superior Nemesio Salcedo opposed such approvals, and thereby countermanded the King's royal order of March 1804.

In 1799, Elguezábal decreed against merchandise from Louisiana coming into Texas. The Marqués de Casa Calvo told Elguezábal in March 1800, that he had prohibited it, also, and had ordered the arrest of all unlicensed traders found among the Arkansas. Commandant general Felipe de Neve told Elguezábal that the commandants at Nacogdoches were to be changed every four to five months in order to prevent them from becoming too intimate with the smugglers and intruders and too lax in enforcing laws against contraband trade. At Rapides, the commandant Valentin Layssard published Casa Calvo's order to arrest and to deport all Americans. "Many without permits of the government are here. I am not capable of answering for their conduct. Americans who are here without passports, without express permission to settle here, or who have not been established here for one year, must leave."

Gayoso, in warning Viceroy Miguel José de Azanza of the dangerous position of Louisiana late in 1798, compared the incursions of Anglo-Americans to the activities of destructive insects:

> "They introduce themselves in the thickness of the forests, like the Indians; they enter particularly via the Colorado and Blanco rivers; they penetrate to the settlements of Attakapas, Opelousas, Natchitoches, San Antonio, reaching to the province of Texas, and I do not doubt that they intend to get farther. First they become acquainted with the Indians, trade with them, and afterwards engage in contraband trade with the natives of Mexico. Some stay in the territories. It won't be long before they will have establishments from which it will not be easy to remove them. They are settled in sufficient numbers so that they will establish their customs, laws, and religion. They will form independent states, aggregating themselves to the Federal Union, which will not refuse to receive them, and progressively they will go as far as the Pacific Ocean. The communication of Illinois with Mexico is already known."

After 1800, the Spanish began to receive word of Anglo-American activity to the north of Santa Fe, and of a British expedition from Canada in 1801. The governor of Santa Fe organized a group of Ute and genízaro spies and sent them among the Kiowa, Ai, Arapaho, and Pawnee to keep Spain informed of Anglo-American activity. And in June 1800, Chacón dispatched a party under Josef Miguel, to examine the territory between New Mexico and Missouri. By then, however, the protective buffer so desired by Spain had become a dangerous open wedge.

Local Spanish officials had taken many precautionary measures, not only military in nature. Attempts had been made to attract immigrants to Spanish Louisiana. Godoy's adage that you cannot lock up an open field had proved true before 1803. God and the foreign office had not protected Spain's frontier in Louisiana. With boundaries yet unmarked, the retrocession of Louisiana to France and its subsequent sale to the United States in 1803 revived all of the old problems of foreign intrusion. Spanish officials in Mexico and Spain perceived too late the importance of frontier officials' earlier proposal for fixing the definite boundaries of Louisiana and Texas at the Sabine.

IV

The purchase of Louisiana increased the fear of American aggression, and the Spaniards therefore tried to prevent the sale. When that failed, Spain tried to restrict the boundaries of the newly purchased territory through diplomacy. Yrujo protested the sale of Louisiana to the United States, but President Madison told him to carry his complaints to France. Spain thus gave up its opposition to the sale of Louisiana the United States, and turned to carrying out a policy of defense on the southwestern border. As implemented, this policy on the Louisiana-Texas frontier consisted of: (1) forbidding all foreigners to cross the frontier (even refusing to permit a former agent from colonizing in Texas, and arresting trader Baptiste La Lande who entered New Mexico); (2) colonizing Texas; (3) establishing garrisons with forts on Matagorda Bay and at Orcoquisac at the mouth of the Trinity, and bringing up reinforcements; and (4) launching expeditions to gain control of the Indians, to impede American settlement, and to intercept United States exploring expeditions. An example of the latter was the use of a Spanish force under Francisco Viana from Nacogdoches to stop an American expedition led by Lieutenant Freeman to the Caddo villages on the Red River.

The United States, too, was active. Some Americans were ready to take forcible possession of Louisiana if necessary. United States Infantry Captain Edward Turner was sent to Natchitoches to watch the frontier, where there was a good deal of friction over land titles and fugitive slaves. And Dr. John Sibley, a surgeon and acting Indian agent at Natchitoches, collected information from the Indians and traders.

The problems facing Spanish Texas after the Louisiana Purchase were similar to those that Spain had faced in Louisiana. American settlers included peaceful ranchers and farmers, deserters from the United States army, and fugitive slaves. Spain was most suspicious of deserters, who might already be, or could become, spies. The boundary with Louisiana was not only undefined and unsettled, but the United States had even wished to include Texas in the purchase of Louisiana. To clarify the situation, in March 1804, the Council of State in Madrid drew this boundary at the Gulf of Mexico, along the Arroyo Hondo to Natchitoches, and up the Red River. Casa Calvo protested American settlements west of the Sabine, and the Spaniards turned back William Dunbar's exploring trip in 1804. A census, however, revealed a goodly number of foreigners still living west of Natchitoches, in Nacogdoches, and in other parts of eastern Texas.

Nemesio Salcedo y Salcedo, commandant general of the Interior Provinces who, as mentioned above, opposed immigration of Americans into Texas, feared that the real purpose of Pike's exploratory expedition of 1806-07 was to subvert the loyalty of the Plains Indians. Salcedo ordered a military expedition from San Antonio to Santa Fe to impress the Indians, especially the Comanche. Salcedo also said that the Embargo Act, which hindered the operations and receipt of supplies by merchants William Barr and Peter Samuel Davenport was to stop goods that Texas needed for Indian presents. Governor Antonio Cordero y Bustamante of Texas even suggested that the inundation by vagrants was a plot on the part of the United States to take the land.

Yet the loss of Louisiana was not as great a threat to the Provincias Internas of New Spain as were its undetermined boundaries. The Spaniards believed that the young United States

Republic had an imperialistic complex and hence they made frantic efforts to encircle the United States with obstacles to expansion. The Spaniards held opposite views of Louisiana's value as a barrier. One view was that Louisiana formed a barrier to its Mexican dominions against the expansionist Westerners. The other was that as a military post, Louisiana was too extensive and too weak for Spain to control effectively.

Both the United States and Spain made exaggerated claims for the boundaries of Louisiana, and both appealed to history and geography to substantiate their claims. But, the boundary was, in practice, between old Natchitoches and old Los Adaes. Proposals for a neutral ground were made early. The first was officially set forth by Secretary of State James Madison in 1804. The movement of forces on both sides, as well as their determination to use armed force, if necessary, led to unofficial recognition of the neutral area between the Sabine and the Arroyo Hondo. The U.S. General Wilkinson and the Spanish Colonel Herrera made an informal agreement to this effect which did not change until Spain yielded to the United States in 1819.

There were two main roads across the Neutral Ground—the old Spanish trail from Natchitoches to Nacogdoches, and the Opelousas road. Two other important but lesser roads ran from Bayou Pierre to Nacogdoches, and from Bayou to Natchitoches. The Neutral Ground proved a weak barrier to the westward advance of the American frontiersman. American and Spanish settlers poured into the area, as did bandits, fugitive slaves, outlaws, and future filibusters and squatters. Inhabitants of the area were both permanent and transient—the latter category including persons unlawfully operating in the area, operating as seasonal farmers, hunters, trappers, guides, highwaymen, and filibusters.

The Neutral Ground was the bridge over which most of the trade between Texas and American Louisiana passed. Spain had prohibited commercial intercourse with American Louisiana, but necessity forced frontier officials to amend the orders. Spain's restrictive policy was replaced by a highly profitable smuggling trade. Barr and Davenport, for example, operated profitably until the Magee-Gutiérrez filibustering expedition invaded Texas in 1812. Thus, the old Franco-Spanish contest for the control of the Indian trade of East Texas and Western Louisiana, as well as for the control and influence of those Indians, continued as an American-Spanish contest. Smuggling could not be stopped: the need for articles of trade was great and the border was wide. Spanish patrols were active, but smugglers were more active. Gradually, as the revolutionary movements in other parts of the Spanish empire distracted the attention of Spanish patrols from the Louisiana border, and as the need for Louisiana articles became acute, commercial restrictions were violated with impunity by settlers and soldiers alike. As a result of complaints about bandits by the merchants of Natchitoches, in 1810 a joint U.S.-Spanish expedition led by Lieutenant Augustus Magee attempted to rid the Neutral Ground area of them.

The Indians living in the area were also an obstacle to American westward expansion. In a tug-of-war the Spaniards worked intensively to maintain Indian allegiance, while the Americans exerted equal effort to win their friendship. The Spaniards encouraged Indians under American jurisdiction to immigrate to Spanish territory and actively opposed attempts of American traders to establish commercial relations with the Indians. Spanish governors held conferences with Indian chiefs and sent emissaries and messages, as well as lavish gifts from their warehouse in San Antonio, to them.

The Americans too were active. Dr. John Sibley, the American Indian agent, encouraged Indians to come to Natchitoches for presents. His agents obtained peltries and horses from the Indians, and Sibley himself maintained a large volume of trade with the Indians from his trading post in Natchitoches.

For a time, the Americans seemed to be gaining the advantage. While the Americans had a well-organized Office of Indian Affairs with factories (trading posts) for every group of Indians, the Spaniards had only the firm of Barr and Davenport, and a few individual traders and trappers to supply the Indian trade. Moreover, all Spanish traders were bound by numerous trade restrictions and by the general prohibition of trade with Louisiana. Once again the Spaniards urged bolstering the Indian barrier to hold back the American westward tide, and colonizing Texas, before the Americans invaded it. They also attempted to capture and keep the trade with the Indians, establishing a trading post at Bayou Pierre and suggesting establishment of a trading factory in

San Antonio. But private enterprise failed due to both lack of capital and lack of government support, as demonstrated in the case of Marcelo Soto at Bayou Pierre. Barr and Davenport were far more successful.

The Interior Provinces had been organized as a separate unit to secure New Spain against the Indians; it now had to be converted into an unstable bulwark against the Anglo-Americans. Of the four interior provinces—New Mexico, Texas, Coahuila, and Nueva Vizcaya—the first two had to bear the brunt of any hostile irruption. In order to guard Texas and New Mexico, three areas had to be protected: (1) the coast of Texas and Nuevo Santander, (2) the Natchitoches-Nacogdoches trail to San Antonio, and (2) the trails leading to Santa Fe from the Red, Arkansas, and Missouri rivers. Nacogdoches became the important focal point just as New Orleans and St. Louis had been previously.

Both the Anglo-Americans and the Spaniards closely watched the movements of the other since interminable rumors had made suspicion the common denominator in their relations. Spaniards were fearful of American filibustering expeditions to attack and conquer the Kingdom of Mexico. As Pierre Clément Laussat wrote on March 27, 1804, in his *Mémoire of my life to my son*, "The United States has voyageurs ascending the Missouri; others covering land routes of Louisiana; they openly wager that they will have a port open on the Pacific Ocean in less than five years. The United States will before long give much trouble to Spain—their purchase of Louisiana has stimulated their ambitions." In 1806 the viceroy received warning from New Orleans that there was a strong party in Louisiana whose object it was to seize the Kingdom of Mexico. The commandant of Nacogdoches indicated that he believed Spain was in imminent danger of losing New Spain to the United States. An "Association to free Mexico" had been established in New Orleans in January 1814. Also called "Association of Friends of Mexican Emancipation," its goal was actually the emancipation of Texas. The principal object of the Aaron Burr conspiracy seems to have been the invasion of Mexico. Burr and Wilkinson studied the maps of Mexico in 1805 and subsequently, Wilkinson and John Adair discussed such an invasion. Carlos Howard in 1806 noted that the preparations of the Americans against the Provincias Internas "are already *tan notorios.*" The governors of the Provincias

Internas repeatedly requested reinforcements. As late as 1806 many citizens in Louisiana expected Spain to regain control of the area purchased by the United States.

Because of the suspicions and rumors of Anglo-American invasion, Salcedo did not relax his vigilance when the Neutral Ground agreement was signed. After 1808, Salcedo took even greater precautions because fear of aggression by Napoleon and by the English was added to the longstanding threat of United States invasion. When Joseph Bonaparte took over in Spain, he sent agents to Mexico, and when his agent, the Frenchman Octaviano D'Alvimar, arrived in Nacogdoches as representative to Spain, he was arrested. Salcedo also stopped communication and trade, telling the viceroy that "the greatest question of the times is the holding of Texas—the buffer state—against the Americans."

But American filibustering expeditions increased. Valentin Foronda, Spanish chargé d'affaires at Philadelphia, warned the comandante general of the Provincias Internas, on January 6, 1809, to watch for activities against New Spain. Governor Vicente Folch y Juan of West Florida also warned the officials, especially his superior at Havana, the Marqués de Someruelos. The latter, captain-general of Cuba and the Floridas, in turn decided that the viceroy of Mexico should take immediate steps to guard Texas, Louisiana, Florida, and the whole of New Spain. José Vidal, commandant at Natchitoches also warned of Anglo-American activities along the border. Beginning in 1810, as in Mexico, violent disturbances shook both east and west of New Orleans; rebellions took place in Texas. Louisiana was a hotbed of conspiracies.

When the Spanish declaration of war against France in 1808 became known in the Provincias Internas, forces were increased and a council was held in San Antonio at which the old, usual recommendations were made: (1) strengthen the garrison at Nacogdoches; (2) increase the overall number of troops; and (3) encourage immigrants to settle the area between the Sabine and San Antonio. Nemesio Salcedo, however, was opposed to the recommendations, especially the third, for he distrusted foreigners. In Texas, during the last decade of Spanish control, 1810-21, there were, as Odie B. Faulk has described, "shadowy conspiracies and actual invasions; bloody revolts, bloodless counter-revolution; comic opera humor and tragic seriousness; years of confusion, unrest and change: Texas was indeed under a 'Green Flag'. To catalogue the dvents and invaders, filibusters and bandits, pseudo-imperialists is unnecessary" for all had "swords for their passport."

Salcedo also informed Pedro Cevallos, Spain's foreign secretary, in 1809, of the need for carefully selecting and strengthening a point or post on the New Mexico frontier with the United States. Such a post could serve as a point of reunion, maintain a sufficient military force to stop any enemy in the interior, and during peacetime prepare *poblaciones* in the entire province to prevent any violation of Spanish territory.

Spain tried to regain Louisiana at the negotiations at Ghent in 1814. The London press boasted that the United States would be chastised and forced to return Louisiana to Spain. However, a diplomatic victory for the United States occurred instead, her territories taken during the War of 1812 being restored. Spain, in turn, brought the matter up at the Congress of Vienna, again without success.

In her attempts to regain Louisiana, Spain consistently endeavored to carry out a policy of defensive reexpansion. Spanish minister Luis de Onís constantly sought reinforcements for Florida and Texas, and tried to keep boundaries as far as possible from the Provincias Internas. Onís was instructed late in 1814 by the restored government of Ferdinand VII to solicit the return of Louisiana on the pretext that France had had no right to sell it. But Onís, who had been rebuffed when he had offered the same argument at the time of the sale (Spain had then told him to stop complaining), understood the realities of the situation and refrained from even presenting the suggestion. Onís instead reported a scheme proposed by Louis de Clouet, former Spanish consul at New Orleans, to recapture Louisiana by force with Spanish troops. In 1817, Arsène Lacarrière Latour, who had been principal military engineer for Andrew Jackson in 1815, was sent by the Spanish, under the alias of John Williams to Havanna to argue the need for defense of Texas against the Americans. He argued that the Americans favored and were aiding the pro-independence insurgents, especially in Louisiana. Keeping with tradition, he suggested establishing forts and promoting colonization attracting Louisiana creoles to Texas. The commandant of the Provincias Internas supported "William's" plan to establish a buffer against the Americans. But nothing came of it. In 1817, the Spanish vice-consul in New Orleans, Felipe Fatio, suggested to the governor of Texas that Irish settlers from Kentucky and Tennessee be located in Texas. Fatio mentioned the possible attempt by Americans, specifically the expedition planned by Colonel John O'Fallon, to occupy or invade Spanish territory. He also warned the governor that certain bands were collecting at Galveston, Trinity, Sabine, Natchez, and Natchitoches and were planning to attack Texas in September 1819. Fatio did not believe that the United States government was involved, since the United States had abandoned Texas by the Treaty of 1819. However no forceful attempts to conquer Texas were made. Spain maintained consuls at New Orleans, St. Louis, Natchez, and Natchitoches, and in other American cities, to observe United States and expatriate Mexican rebel activities. Opinion in Louisiana, however, became violently anti-Spanish, and the Spanish Vice-consul Diego Morphy in New Orleans was once seriously hurt when hit over the head with an umbrella. Spain lodged a complaint and demanded protection for Spanish agents by the United States government.

During the complicated and prolonged American negotiations with Spain between 1816 and 1819, many proposals were made. These included a Spanish suggestion to trade Florida to England in exchange for help in conquering Louisiana; and the cession of Florida to the United States in exchange for Louisiana territory claimed by the United States west of the Mississippi (with New Orleans to be retained by the United States). This latter proposal was made by Spain in 1817 as an attempt to protect her Provincias Internas. In fact, when Casa Calvo and Salcedo learned of the Louisiana Purchase, they advised Spain to negotiate another treaty with the United States by which the Mississippi River would become the international boundary. They felt that Spain could safely exchange Baton Rouge and part of West Florida for American territory west of the Mississippi. It was declined by the United States. It is true that by the Adams-Onís Treaty of 1819 Florida was ceded to the United States and the purchase of Louisiana recognized, but with the western boundary running along the Sabine and Red rivers. In the last analysis, the western, or Louisiana-Texas boundary, was set where it had always been in common usage. Spain, still fearing United States actions, delayed ratifying the treaty, and during that delay popular sentiment in the United States urged the seizure of both Florida and Texas. But

President James Monroe and Secretary of State John Adams urged patience, knowing that seizure might bring on trouble with England. James Long's filibustering expedition of 1819, which culminated in the taking of Nacogdoches and a subsequent declaration of independence for Texas before being put down by Spanish troops, exemplified prevailing anti-Spanish sentiment in Louisiana.

Onís realized that Spain could reap but little advantage from the treaty if colonists were not placed along the frontier and on the coast. Onís thus proposed plans for colonies, advocated colonization, and also asked for land. A buffer state settled by Swiss and Germans was suggested. In 1821, shortly before exchange of ratifications of the Adams-Onís Treaty, Moses Austin's colonization plan to settle three hundred families on land grants in Texas was accepted by the Texas governor Antonio Martinez. These events coincided with the settlement of the last frontier of Spanish Louisiana, and with the eviction of Spain, following Mexican independence, from North America. Although border problems continued, Spain was succeeded by the newly independent Mexico in ownership of the former Provincias Internas. The Anglo-Spanish conflict over the western borderlands gave way to a Mexican-American conflict, one which would continue until the westward expansion of the United States had reached to the Pacific Ocean.

7

The Last Frontier:
North from Santa Fe

While Spain and Mexico were undergoing those revolutionary changes that would destroy the Spanish empire in North America, the United States was rapidly expanding west to the Rocky Mountains. Under the treaty of the purchase of Louisiana, the United States claimed West Florida, and Texas, and seemed also to include Oregon; at least the United States laid some fuzzy claims to all that area. Spain argued that those areas had not been included in the Louisiana Purchase, and during the negotiations between Adams and Onís, lasting from 1817 to 1819, more than eleven proposals concerning ownership and division of the area were ventured, discussed, and debated.

Prior to the 1819 Adams-Onís settlement, both Spain and the United States claimed the area between Santa Fe and St. Louis, and the contest for control was often more than verbal. Spain attempted, for example, to incite the Indians against the United States. She also sought to exclude United States citizens from the area and opposed official and military expeditions, even exploratory ones. She prohibited American trade with Texas and New Mexico. Some American traders did reach Santa Fe, but most suffered penalties. Spain not only kept a watchful eye on the Lewis and Clark expedition but attempted to prevent it at the outset, claiming that, although St. Louis might be within the area purchased by the United States, the territory beyond (where the Missouri turns from its approximately north-south direction) was outside the limits of the Louisiana Purchase. Hence, claimed the Spanish, the expedition's route along the upper parts of the Missouri River through present day Montana and across the mountains intruded upon Spanish territory.

The lack of precise boundaries for Louisiana had always handicapped Spanish officials in Louisiana and the Provincias Internas. Beginning in the 1780s, the Spanish watched closely the overland explorations of Americans and other foreigners. They reported on President Thomas Jefferson's interest in exploration, on André Michaux's 1793 proposed expedition (funded by the American Philosophical Society) to the Pacific, and on Jefferson's appointment of Meriwether Lewis, to undertake a "literary" expedition (i.e., to gather geographical and zoological information). As noted above, the Spaniards were displeased with the Lewis and Clark expedition largely because they considered it an invasion of a Spanish province. "If we wish to maintain unharmed the dominions of the King and prevent the ruin and destruction of the Provincias Internas," wrote the Marquis of Casa Calvo, Spain's commissioner of boundaries, and Manuel de Salcedo to Nemesio Salcedo, "the only thing to do would be to arrest Captain Merry Wheather and his party which can hardly avoid passing among the Indian nations neighboring New Mexico, its presidios, or rancherías. Decisive action must be taken against them to cut short the countless disagreements which must originate between the two governments." The Louisiana officials asked the commandant of the Provincias Internas to act forthwith, arrest the expedition's members and confiscate their papers, on the grounds that the line of demarcation had yet to be determined. "The Americans," they argued, "cannot infer that it already belongs to the United States; they, however, publicly even claim to the Rio Grande and their repeated designs and incursion have the same objectives and purposes as [had] Philip Nolan." Thus orders went out from Jaoquin del Real Alencaster, governor of New Mexico, to Pedro Vial on October 13, 1805, to investigate the Lewis and Clark expedition, to arrest its members, even to arouse Indian hostility. Spanish expeditions reconnoitred between New Mexico and the Missouri River, seeking to secure the alliance of Indian tribes. A party of Comanche reconnoitred the country as far as the banks of the Missouri, with orders from Governor Alencaster of New Mexico, to determine whether the Lewis expedition had penetrated Spanish territory, and, if so, to turn it back.

The Spaniards also opposed the Jeffersonian explorations of the Red and Arkansas rivers. Visiting the Panana (Pawnee) to check on the Lewis and Clark expedition, Vial discovered that of all the

Indian tribes in the area only the Pawnee remained loyal to Spain. Nemesio Salcedo, commandant general of the Interior Provinces, informed the governor at Santa Fe that Lewis and Clark were distributing gifts, goods, and firearms to the Indians, possibly to incite them to war against the Spaniards. Salcedo therefore ordered the governor to cultivate the Pawnee and to acquire the friendship of the Oto and Lobo as well as other Indian nations of the Missouri, Platte, and Arkansas rivers. The governor was to send presents, invite the chiefs to Santa Fe, appoint Juan Chalvert (who "has been of good conduct, truth, and desirous of giving proof of usefulness") as the new interpreter to the Pawnee, encourage Indian hatred of the English and Americans, seize Lewis and Clark on their return voyage, and even invite potentially good Spanish subjects from Louisiana to settle in Nueva Vizcaya. Salcedo defined the limits of his jurisdiction as extending from New Mexico to the Illinois settlements, from the Mississippi and Missouri possessions to the English possessions in Canada, and specifically included the tributaries of the Missouri and Platte rivers. Perhaps Nemesio Salcedo was incorporating too much, for he based his decision on old French documents.

Later, upon orders from Spain, Salcedo called for the arrest of all Americans found among the Indian nations but avoided including Lewis and Clark in this category. He continued to give orders to strengthen the friendship of Indians inhabiting the banks of the Missouri and others, and to acquire all possible information on the area between New Mexico and Upper Louisiana. Conversely, one of the objectives of the Lewis and Clark expedition was to cultivate those same Indians. The Americans thus turned the tables and began to keep a watchful eye on Spanish Indian policy. Pierre Chouteau, Sr., for example, informed President Jefferson of Spanish intrigues with the Indians and of the attempts by the Spanish government to create intimate ties with the nations of the Missouri.

Although the Spanish had known from the beginning that Lewis might go to the sea, they made no move against him on the coast. Not until the return trip did Spain lodge official protests with the American government. They may have missed their best opportunity. The province of New Mexico could have sent a force against the expedition, but in 1806 the Spaniards were obviously less certain of their jurisdiction than they would be thirteen years later when they claimed the Yellowstone area. Each official in the upper echelons of the Spanish hierarchy waited for someone else to assume the awesome responsibility of stopping Lewis and Clark.

For many years there had been reports into Santa Fe of considerable activity by foreigners among the Indians of the Osage, Kansas, Republican, and Platte rivers. Actually there had been little movement of Anglos or others from the Missouri toward Santa Fe before Lewis and Clark, although Americans had been infiltrating Texas, the Arkansas River area, and the Osage country. Lewis and Clark who believed that neither long distances nor rough mountains separated the drainage of the Upper Missouri from New Mexico, confirmed this in their minds when they noticed Spanish horses among the Shoshoni and Nez Perce Indians. Reports of United States army officers in 1804 described *Spanish* traders moving up the mountains of the headwaters of the Platte to trade with Americans who used to hunt there.

Beginning about 1804, however, the situation changed, and traders penetrated the region in ever increasing numbers. Their names and the details of their activities need not concern us here, but it is clear that, following the Lewis and Clark expedition, the Americans wasted no time in making tracks in the direction of Santa Fe. From 1803 to the time of Pike, the adventurers, travelers, and traders bore French names, but most of these men financed by Morrison, Loisel, Lisa, Clamorgan, and other fur traders and merchants operating out of St. Louis, had become U.S. nationals after 1803. From the American standpoint, it was clearly Lewis and Clark who provided the impetus to expansion. Returning with detailed geographical information and with tantalizing stories of trading opportunities, they ignited the inflammable Anglo-American imagination and inspired Americans who dreamt of getting rich quickly and easily.

Most of the problems on this last frontier stemmed from the imprecise boundaries of the Louisiana Purchase, as well as from inaccurate maps and lands still unsurveyed, if indeed, not officially explored. Claims and counterclaims were common, for the Spanish were deeply concerned with the future of New Mexico. Spanish fear for the safety of the remainder of her empire in North America was due in part to the fact that the lines of communication between the United States and New Mexico and Texas were open and accessible for that day and age. Various rivers connected New

Mexico and American possessions, and were an invitation to aggressive frontiersmen and traders to accept the challenge of penetrating the remaining Spanish provinces. Reporting in 1809 from San Antonio, Governor Manuel de Salcedo delineated American ambitions and designs. Between the United States and New Mexico and Texas, six easy routes were open. The Missouri-Platte rivers carried travelers as far west as present-day Colorado; the Arkansas River reached within a short distance of Santa Fe; from St. Louis there was a straight road to Natchitoches and Texas; and there was a route to Texas from the Arkansas and Ouachita rivers; the Red River passed through Natchitoches and penetrated far into the interior of New Mexico; and finally, there was the route from the Pawnee and Caddo nations, through Bayou Pierre to Nacogdoches.

It was therefore incumbent upon Spain to outbid the Americans and increase trade with the Indian nations. New presidios to keep the Indians of Texas within the Spanish hold were required, especially since the worst crime of those Indians was to steal horses and mules. The Spanish considered an attempt at preventing American occupation of Louisiana, but that was quickly dismissed as an idle dream. Spain therefore resorted to the policy of trying to restrict Louisiana to the narrowest possible boundaries while strenghtening the New Mexico defenses. Nemesio Salcedo wrote Pedro Cevallos to this effect on March 7, 1809. New Mexico now entered what proved to be a seventeen-year period of anxiety. Americans did little to assuage Spanish insecurity. Intrusions quickly followed announcement of the Louisiana Purchase. Most were not official United States expeditions of the Lewis and Clark variety; rather, they generally consisted of adventurous parties seeking commercial profit. Although these private efforts posed no inherent military threat, the Spanish realized that these firstcomers often constituted the vanguard of imperialism. Indeed, the Lewis and Clark expedition had reaffirmed, in the Spanish mind, such a threat.

The New Mexicans, therefore, stepped up their activities among the Plains Indians. Confident of Comanche loyalty, they concentrated on extending their influence to the north and east. But Pedro Vial and Juan Chalvert failed to pacify the Pawnee: failure of the Vial-Chalvert expedition which was attacked by hostile Indians in the vicinity of the Arkansas River was a great disappointment. Additional soldiers were needed for future expeditions said Vial, as was a fort on the Arkansas River. Spanish officials, however, remained confident of gaining the allegiance of the Indians through gifts instead of through force. Juan Lucero, an associate of Pedro Vial, was sent to visit the Kiowa and Comanche and secured their alliance. In 1805, Joaquin del Real Alencaster, governor of New Mexico, begged for reinforcements, especially when he learned of some disaffection among the Cuampa and Pawnee. He agreed with Vial's recommendation for a fort on the Arkansas to deal with the Indians as far away as the Missouri, encouraged granting medals and goods to counter American activity among those Indians, and suggested stationing interpreters among the tribes. A second Vial-Chalvert expedition was sent out in 1806, but failed to extend Spanish influence to the Missouri River.

A greater potential danger to Spanish New Mexico was the Zebulon Pike expedition, news of which came to Nemesio Salcedo from Spanish spies in St. Louis. The Spanish countered by commissioning a military expedition headed by Facundo Melgares to intercept Lieutenant Freeman's expedition up the Red River (in case it eluded the Spanish force sent from Nacogdoches). Melgares was, moreover, to reconnoitre the area from New Mexico to the junction of the Platte and Missouri rivers; to ply the Indians with presents; and to attempt to locate Pike. He held a successful council with the Comanche on the Red River. Shortly thereafter, he arranged a treaty with the Pawnee who did agree to prevent passage of Americans through their lands. (Nonetheless they stole some of Melgares' horses.) But Pike finessed the Spanish, arriving among the Pawnee after Melgares' departure and, because of his aggressive spirit and impressive forces, neutralizing them. Pike's victory, however, was only momentary, for the Spanish some time later arrested him and took him to Santa Fe. Spanish officialdom was, by this time, thoroughly alarmed, and instructions flowed into the offices of the Spanish provincial governors. Alencaster, on orders, revised his defensive plan for New Mexico. He would maintain reconnaissance parties to observe the frontiers of New Mexico and to warn of American approaches. The New Mexico borderland had been somewhat reduced, and instead of the former plan to meet the American advance on the plains, or if possible at the Missouri River, New Mexico would now meet and deal with the intruders in the intermediate environs of New Mexico or even within the borders of the province itself. Such strategy was obviously self-defeating.

Another interesting borderland affair is sometimes connected with the Pike story. All during the later period of Spanish colonial rule attempts to reach Santa Fe from Missouri had been contemplated, if not actually made. By use of Indian tribes, indirect arrangements for passage had been established, especially after the epoch-making journey of Pedro Vial. Although theoretically direct trade was prohibited by law, the lure of Santa Fe and of profits from Indian trading and other commerce spurred on the efforts of traders, especially those from St. Louis. These efforts eventually reached fruition, but not until after the actual transfer of Louisiana to the United States. We have seen that several of the traders from St. Louis who ascended the Missouri in the very early years of the nineteenth century actually surfaced in Santa Fe. Merchants who had been the leading traders with St. Louis under the Spanish regime did not alter course simply because the change of ownership of Louisiana. They continued their efforts. In September, 1806, when the returning Lewis and Clark were only a week's journey from Saint Louis, they met John McClallen, an ex-army officer turned fur trader, who had been sent on a speculative trip by James Wilkinson, to New Spain with a view to introducing trade with the inhabitants. MaClallen hoped that the Oto and Pawnee would guide him. Wilkinson, of course, was a master intriguer and always had his hand in anything that gave promise of profit. The older traders, as for example, Manuel Lisa, who had been given the chance to trade among the Osage Indians in the later years of Spanish rule, also had trade with New Mexico in mind, even after he jumped into the lucrative and virgin field of fur trade of the Upper Missouri upon the return and report of Lewis and Clark. Lisa and Wilkinson were not on good terms, and the former attempted to thwart some of Wilkinson's activities and trade. Lisa's intent was to neutralize American interest in the Osage-Pawnee-Comanche country and link Spanish alliance with those tribes to his plan to establish a three-cornered trade among the Indians, St. Louis, and Santa Fe. On August 29, 1806, Lisa was granted a license by Frederick Bates, acting superintendent of Indian Affairs in St. Louis to trade with the Republican Nation of Indians residing on the Osage River, with authorization to use one barge and eight men, and to sell, barter, and exchange all manner of goods, wares, and merchandise in those Indians' own towns. In 1807, Lisa procured a further license to trade on the Missouri with the Pawnee Indians in amity with the United States. Jacques Clamorgan was licensed to trade with the Pani (thereby giving him a ruse to enter upon his larger scheme of trade with Santa Fe). Lisa and Clamorgan formed a partnership, purchased goods, and Clamorgan undertook the journey to Santa Fe. In 1807, they also started a barge load of goods toward New Mexico escorted by a party commanded by Louison Baudin. Clamorgan's expedition was successful, the only one to make a profio, jnd return. Both Pike and Wilkinson had suspected Lisa's interest in St. Louis-Santa Fe trade; they now knew it to be a fact. Jacques Clamorgan, the man who repeatedly failed to blaze the trail made famous by Lewis and Clark, actually became the first to make a trading venture into Santa Fe and to return to Missouri with his profits. Clamorgan did not repeat his efforts but did describe his journeys in the *Missouri Gazette*, as well as expound on the commerce of the region.

American intrusions became an increasingly grave problem in New Mexico, and the Spanish correspondingly stepped up reconnaissance activities and their cultivation of Indians allies. Juan Lucero who had secured Indian allies for Spain in 1805, now visited the Comanche to find out about intruding foreign hunters and traders. Special consideration was to be given the Comanche, since they were New Mexico's most loyal and numerous allies and, because of their location, the most valuable in preventing surprise approaches to the province. Governor José Manrrique also continued to grant licenses to New Mexican residents to trade with the tribes with the idea that traders could observe Indian conduct, as well as report the appearance of foreigners to Santa Fe.

Reports about American intruders, chiefly from the Comanche and Kiowa, continued to flow into Santa Fe. One concerned a very large party of Americans who were constructing a fort at the confluence of the Río del Almagre (Fountain Creek, Colorado) and the Arkansas River. A reconnoitring-expedition failed to confirm that report although it did verify the presence of small parties of Americans on the Platte. Precautionary measures were taken when rumor had it that the Americans were attempting to induce the Comanches to join them in an attack on New Mexico. From Washington the Marquis de Casa Yrujo repeatedly warned Spanish officials of impending American invasions. For example, on December 20, 1805, he wrote Casa Calvo and Viceroy Iturrigaray (and the information filtered down to officials in both New Mexico and Spain) that Indians, some with intimate knowledge of Santa Fe and other Spanish settlements in the vicinity, were being brought to Washington. He enclosed extracts from Louisville newspapers telling of a considerable detachment of troops already on the way to form an establishment "near the coast of Santa Fe, and a large reinforcement is to be joined them in the spring, which will effectually extend and protect our peltry trade, and open a safe and easy communication with the Dons."

Misinformation infected both sides. The Spaniards suspected that trappers might be "spies." In the winter of 1809-10 a party from St. Louis headed by James Patterson, Reuben Smith, and Joseph McLanahan was placed under arrest when the men reached Santa Fe. Their goods were confiscated and the trio imprisoned. American newspapers in Philadelphia and Louisiana editorialized against the "butchery" by the Spaniards. While the men were in jail, a party of eight rescuers led by a former U.S. Army officer, Captain Walker, was restrained by the Osage Indians and held for American authorities. Walker reportedly said that his group would be joined, at the confluence of the Canadian and Arkansas rivers, by three hundred armed Kentuckians, who would then march down to Chihuahua to free the Patterson group, and, incidentally, seize any gold they could find. The Patterson men were freed after a year and returned to Natchitoches, where they joined the Magee-Gutierrez filibustering "Green Flag" expedition that tried to free Texas from Spain, late in 1812. Soon after their return, the Patterson men, especially McLanahan, wrote letters announcing their intent to go back to Mexico. When Secretary of State James Monroe heard of this he wrote to Governor Benjamin Howard of Louisiana Territory on September 3, 1812, repudiating the idea and proclaiming it illegal. McLanahan later admitted that his treatment had not been as bad as reported, that he had entered the Provincias Internas for the sole purpose of obtaining geographical and commercial information, that he had been well aware of Spanish opposition to such intrusions, but that he had been apprehended on the headwaters of the Red River, an area claimed by the United States.

A story of a strange borderland affair now seems in order. It involved Manuel Lisa, a Spaniard himself, but one already suspicious in the eyes of Spanish officials. Active in the trade of the Upper Missouri, he had always wanted to establish trade with Santa Fe. In 1810, Luis de Onís (Spanish Bonapartist ambassador to the United States) informed the Viceroy of Mexico, who in turn informed Spanish officials, of Manuel Lisa's proposed expedition of 1811 along the rivers Norte, Grande, Colorado, and Missouri. Onís described Lisa as a "chieftain or spy," who as a result of previous expeditions already knew that country well. Presuming that Lisa might try to surprise New Mexico because of his knowledge of that territory, Onís informed the commandants to be prepared and take the necessary measures. "Watch those men who wish to introduce themselves in the Provincias Internas, bent on any pretext whatever, who do not have a passport from the authorities of His Majesty," he warned. It was, however, in connection with his expedition of 1811 and 1812, that Lisa made his third attempt to open trade with the Spanish. His first attempt had been turned back by Pike; his second consisted of Clamorgan's successful venture which later led to litigation with Lisa. Now came his third—and last.

Lisa was a determined man. Ever since his first journey to the forks of the Missouri he had desired an opportunity to communicate with his Spanish compatriots. From Lisa's fort at the entrance of the Bighorn River, the Indians said, a man on horseback could reach the Spanish settlements on the head of the Del Norte in fourteen days. Lisa sent twenty-three hunters to the Arapaho. They returned to Fort Mandan in 1811 and told him of the annual Spanish visit to Arapaho country. Lisa, therefore, sent out Juan Bautista Champlin and Juan Bautista Lafargue to trade with the Arapaho on the South Platte, and presumably, to make contact with Spanish traders. When some of his hunters failed to arrive at Fort Manuel in 1812, Lisa dispatched some engagés to search for them. They also carried his letter addressed to the Spaniards in which he requested that trade be opened. Later Lisa discovered that the Blackfeet had killed his men—except for one who had joined the Spanish. His nearest approach to establishing good relations came when he ransomed a Spanish boy from the Pawnee Indians, cared for him, and later returned him to his parents. "Humanitarian Lisa," as Ramón Ruiz has said, "might receive Spanish attention, but merchant Don Manuel's men felt harsher treatment." In the end, however, Lisa failed, and never received any favors from New Mexican officials.

While Lisa vainly and somewhat deviously sought to establish trade with New Mexico, others endeavored to do so more directly. Robert McKnight, Samuel Chambers, and James Baird left St. Louis in 1812, to open up trade, anticipating a warm welcome since Hidalgo's *Grito de Dolores* had already occurred. Even before they left, however, Hidalgo's revolt had been crushed, and the American traders received a painful reception in Santa Fe, where they were permitted to meditate in jail over the confiscation of their goods. Other American traders also reached Santa Fe, with similar results. Chief among these was the celebrated August P. Chouteau-Jules de Mun expedition of 1817, whose members were rewarded with imprisonment, court-martial and loss of their goods. Although they were later permitted to leave, their case was the subject of years of diplomatic correspondence. Eventually claims were awarded the heirs of Chouteau and de Mun.

Spanish officials responsible for the security of New Mexico continued to be apprehensive. American activities in Louisiana were increasing, and regardless of their motives, provoked Spanish anxiety. Perhaps the American threat appeared particularly menacing because of the inadequacy of New Mexico's defensive capabilities.

Yet New Mexico's problems remained the same. Most ominous was the news from Minister Onís in 1818 which stated that an American expedition would soon be launched against New Mexico. Rumor had it that emissaries had already been sent out to facilitate the venture, and that some inhabitants of New Mexico, as well as surrounding Indian tribes, were ready to support it. New Mexico sought to escalate its response: the last effort—a defensive attempt to stop and prevent infiltration by parties of Americans—was now to occur. It was to be Spain's last attempt to secure the territory it claimed in the north—to the Missouri or at least to the Yellowstone River. It was also to fail, and, after 1817, the Spanish borderland would become an American frontier.

II

For a long time the area claimed by the Spanish north of Santa Fe was relatively free of foreign intrusions, but Spain was not allowed to ignore the Indians. As late as 1805, Lieutenant-colonel

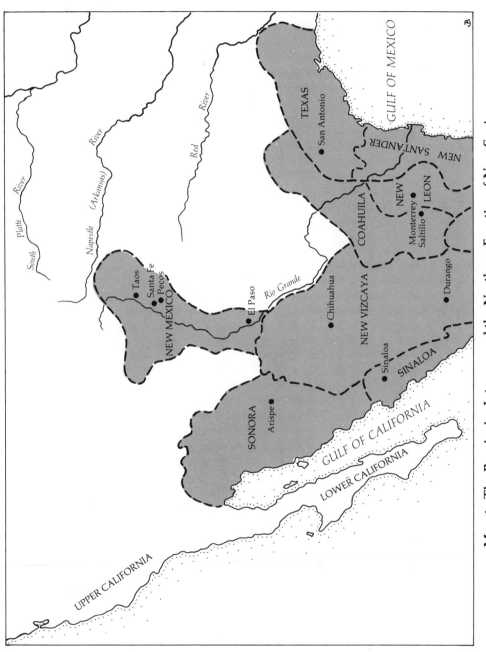

Map 6—The Provincias Internas and the Northern Frontier of New Spain

Antonio Narbona, who was to become governor of New Mexico in 1825, carried on a campaign against the Navajo, and made one of the many Navajo-Spanish peace treaties dating from this period.

Lieutenant Facundo Melgares who had made expeditions to drive out American traders from the country west of the Missouri, had worked to strengthen the alliance between Spaniards and Plains Indians; Juan María de Arce, a lieutenant of Santa Fe, was sent on a scouting expedition towards the Arkansas River to investigate rumors of Anglo-Americans among the Pawnee nations. In 1808, Captain Francisco Amangual, Spanish commandant at La Bahía, made an epic journey, with wheeled vehicles, from San Antonio to Santa Fe to El Paso and back to San Antonio. His expedition visited the Comanche to obtain information about the Anglo-Americans, and to persuade the Indians to assist Spain in keeping out the Americans. Vigilance was the word of the moment. So were trading and exploration. Spanish goods and horses were reaching far into the north country—by means of trade as well as by theft. As early as the 1750s, Arikara and Mandan villages served as trading centers for the northern plains. Spaniards traded, through tribal intermediaries, horses for maize and squash. The English traded guns in return for the same. These same intermediaries carried trade to the Blackfeet in Montana who used goods to pay for horses. The Comanche, Kiowa, Pawnee, Arapaho, and Shoshone were the principal intermediaries in that trade, buying, or if possible, stealing, horses from the Spaniards at Santa Fe or in northern New Mexico.

The Upper Missouri tribes (Arikara, Mandan, and others) were situated by the mid eighteenth century in a most admirable location for trading both towards the northeast, the moving frontier of the horse, and towards the southwest, the moving frontier of the gun. Indian contact with the whites thus produced two major changes in the Indian way of life (and subsequently in their warfare): the use of horses, obtained from the Spaniards, and the use of guns, obtained from the French and British in the northeast. Spanish policy strictly prohibited trading firearms to the Indians. The demand for horses and firearms exceeded the supply.

After 1760, the Spanish directed their attention northward, across western Colorado into the Great Basin, then on to the San Luis Valley. Colorado was, in fact, an outpost of New Mexico, and Santa Fe became the base for Spanish operations in that area: i.e., cultivating Indian friendship, investigating French traders' activities among the Pawnee, and searching for precious metals. The Ute trade, beginning with the Rivera expedition sent out by order of New Mexican Governor Tomás Vélez Cachupín in 1765, reached as far as the Gunnison River. Private traders must have continued after Rivera. But at this juncture the movement was enlarged to encompass the broad Spanish borderland. Due to the Russian advance, the Spaniards occupied Alta California, creating a need for an overland route to Alta California. De Anza's route had not been satisfactory. To find a route, to get acquainted with the Indians of the north and northeast, and to explore, in 1776 the well-known Domínguez-Escalante expedition probed the Great Basin. Although the expedition failed to find the route to California, it did explore the Great Basin, promised a religious mission (which was never carried out) and established trade, with the Indians. De Anza's hard-hitting campaign against the Comanche in 1779—which went north into the San Luis Valley and east to the head of the Arkansas River near Salida, Colorado—was the last official expedition carried out under the Spanish regime. Although de Anza made peace with the Comanche in 1786, Spanish attention temporarily turned from the area due to the war with England which diverted men and money to the Mississippi Valley and the Atlantic Coast. As a result, the problem of protection of California and the Pacific Northwest received more attention.

Indian traders cared little about international affairs and trading expeditions to the north continued. The Ute along the tributaries of the Colorado and the Great Basin, offered good trade opportunities. In 1813, two New Mexicans named Mauricio Arze and Lagos García led a small trading expedition from Abiquiu to the Sevier River in southern Utah.

Spanish officialdom, meanwhile, began to receive word of Anglo-American activity to the north, and in 1801, became fearful of an English invasion from Canada. This persuaded the Spaniards to organize a group of Utes to spy among the Kiowa, Arapaho, and Pawnee in order to keep informed of Anglo-American activity. Spanish traders as well as mountain men like James Workman and Samuel Spencer continued to work among the Ute, and Manuel Mestas (a seventy-year-old genízaro who had reduced the Ute to peace) was paid wages as interpreter. In 1807, two Ute brought Dr.

John H. Robinson, a companion of Pike and possibly his spy, to Governor Alencaster, which resulted in the arrest of Pike's party.

After 1804, Spanish New Mexico's task was to keep the peace with the Ute, the Comanche, and other tribes to the north in order to bolster Spanish claims to that area. The Spaniards were forced to make war on the Navajo but peace was restored after about a year; they also warred with the Apache, with whom they had marked trouble.

But the area between Santa Fe and the Yellowstone and Missouri rivers is vast. In 1816, New Mexican Governor Pedro María Allande sent out numerous reconnaissance parties east to the Arkansas River and to western Arkansas, and north to the Yellowstone River. Pedro Vial, Facundo Melgares, Juan Lucero, and Juan Chalvert were employed to find and bring back information from the Indian, thus keeping the Spaniards in New Mexico well informed, if not entirely secure.

III

The officials of New Mexico were most conscious of the province's vulnerability, and they repeatedly appealed to their superiors, particularly the commandants general of the Provincias Internas for military reinforcements and supplies. The New Mexicans, however, were at a disadvantage, for they had few men, fewer supplies, and not enough presents for the Indians. Little by little Indians were enticed away by American traders and trappers, and even by official agents of the United States government, especially those of the Department of War and of the Superintendency of Indian affairs. Pedro Bautista de Pino, New Mexico's native-born delegate to the Spanish Cortes in 1812, presented an *exposición* to that body detailing New Mexico's problems and proposals for the defense of the province against the American threat. His principal suggestion was to enlarge and reorganize the province's military forces and to establish five presidios. But the Cortes paid little attention to Pino.

From 1816 to 1818, under the governorship of Pedro María de Allande, New Mexico's problems continued. Bernardo Bonavía y Zapata, commandant general in 1809-10, had ordered the New Mexico governor to cultivate the friendship of the Comanche.

Reports that the Eastern Comanche and Anglo-Americans were stealing horses, among other things, prompted the governor to send Juan Lucero on several investigative expeditions, two of them in 1817. Rumor had it that the Anglo-Americans were seducing the Indians with promises in order to persuade them to declare war on the Spaniards, or at least to aid the Americans in invading Mexico. Lucero, however, reported that he found no foreigners, although Americans had visited the Comanche village of Soquequi (or Soquiné) three times, and had been with them on the River de la Huage, where the Comanche chief was carrying on war against the Panana (Pawnee). The commandant general replied to Lucero's report by ordering that, when the Comanche chief, after his Panana campaign, came to Santa Fe, his friendship, which the Spaniards needed more than ever be strongly cultivated. In addition the commandant general ordered the governor of New Mexico to continue to seek peace with the Yamparica Comanche on the borders of New Mexico.

It was under such conditions that New Mexicans received Onís' news that an American expedition would soon be launched against New Mexico. The governor of New Mexico was immediately ordered to prepare his province's defenses for a surprise attack. Captain Facundo Melgares and others were sent out to investigate. From friendly Indians, Governor Allande also received news of foreign hunters on the rivers near New Mexico including the Arkansas River not far from Taos. These foreigners were supposedly giving gunpowder and gifts to the Pawnee, Kiowa, and other tribes, making peace with the Indians, and inviting them to join the Americans in an attack on New Mexico. It was reported that a *fortaleza* had been built by Anglo-Americans on the Napestle [Arkansas] River: *"para reforzarse y atacar a la provincia* [New Mexico]." Allande sent special confidential agents among the tribes to find out news and report but the truth of such activities was elusive.

When an American attack failed to materialize, Facundo Melgares, made acting governor of New Mexico in 1818, turned his attention to the openly hostile Navajo. He prepared for a compaign against them which he planned to lead himself. However, Manuel Cayetano Hernández, a soldier in the presidial company of Carrizal, brought news—once again of an imminent American invasion—to Lieutenant José María de Arce in Taos. Melgares forwent the Navajo campaign to stay in Santa Fe and interrogate Hernández. Meanwhile, Arce alerted frontiersmen to be on their guard, while he went on a reconnaissance mission as far as the Arkansas and Platte rivers. And Juan de Lucero, who had recently visited the Comanche and found no hint of the projected attack, was sent back to hold a council with the Comanche.

Both Melgares and Arce questioned Hernández closely. Melgares confused Hernández in his testimony several times, so much so that it became obvious that news of an imminent American attack was pure fiction. This was reinforced when Lucero returned, accompanied by Comanche who wished to trade, and informed Melgares that there were no more than nineteen Americans currently on the Missouri River.

Arce's expedition also undermined Hernández' tale. Arce had crossed the Sangre de Cristo Mountains and camped on the Huérfano River in Colorado. Parties sent to the Arkansas and to the Platte found nothing. Arce's diary confirmed Commandant general Alejo García Conde's views that the only Americans on the Missouri were the small parties reported by the Comanche. Conde became confident that an American attack was remote: he contended that New Mexico was distant from the American settlements; that Indian tribes could usually be relied upon to provide warning; and finally that New Mexico was capable of defending itself. The Viceroy Juan Ruiz de Apodaca, nonetheless continued to feel that Governor Melgares should gain the friendship of the Pawnee and other tribes as soon as possible. Once again the New Mexicans breathed a sigh of temporary relief.

Distant events also played their part in the Spanish borderlands. Many Napoleonic supporters fled France after the downfall of Napoleon and the Bourbon restoration in France. Some of these exiles were granted land on the Tombigbee River in the southern United States; others were engaged in various political movements. In the summer of 1817, Baron Guillaume Hyde de Neuville, French minister to the United States, received a report of a previously suspected event: French exiles were preparing to attack New Spain, and their probable objective would be New Mexico. Although outside his jurisdiction, he felt that such a move on the part of the Frenchmen might be a source of embarrassment to France, and he acted accordingly. He proposed to Onís that at the cost of the French government, a lieutenant-general well-known for his loyalty, together with a party of twelve to fifteen men under the pretext of hunting be sent through the Provincias Internas to Mexico. Luis de Mun (brother of Jules de Mun) and Edouard Lavaud, volunteered to de Neuville to undertake the mission. The French Minister hired the two men to discover the plans of the French exiles, to warn the Spanish officials, and to dissuade other Frenchmen from participating. Onís, the Spanish Minister, approved the mission and issued Spanish passports to the Frenchmen.

De Mun visited his brother in St. Louis, where he received information about conditions in Santa Fe. He also investigated along the Mississippi to the Arkansas, returned to St. Louis, and later went to Washington. Lavaud, meanwhile, went to New Orleans, met the Bonapartist generals Charles and Henri Lallemand, and witnessed preparations of the French exiles for what was to be their unsuccessful invasion of Texas. He, too, then proceeded to Washington.

Following his return to Washington, de Mun compiled a detailed report on New Mexico and a map, relying chiefly on Pike's journal and his brother's information. His report was a comprehensive indictment of New Mexico's vulnerability. New Mexico's forts were too few, he wrote; too scattered, and too poorly equipped. There was a lack of goods with which to compete with the Americans for influence over the Indian tribes on the northern and eastern borders of New Mexico. There was no doubt that the Indians would become either a means of New Mexican defense, or an instrument of American attack. De Mun described three suitable entry routes through New Mexico's mountain barrier: (1) Sangre de Cristo Pass in present Colorado, reached from the Huérfano, easily accessible but relatively easy to defend; (2) Taos Pass to the south, reached from a branch of the Red River, more difficult of access, but with even better defensive possibilities; and (3) El Vado Pass, about thirty miles southeast of Santa Fe near present San Miguel, New Mexico. De Mun knew little about El Vado, but suspected that it was easy of access. It was also, however, well traveled, making it a poor route for a surprise attack. There was a fourth pass to the north of Sangre de Cristo, but it was poor and little used, even by the Indians. De Mun was convinced that a military expedition from St. Louis could, with relative ease, gain control of New Mexico; all the more so with Indian allies. The New Mexican governor had periodically dispatched parties to reconnoitre the lands east of the mountains, but since they had never encountered enemies they had become negligent, and their militia were poorly armed. De Mun estimated that a well-mounted force could go from St. Louis to Taos, along the Arkansas and Huérfano rivers and through Sangre de Cristo Pass, in from thirty-five to forty days.

Onís sent an unsigned copy of the de Mun report to the viceroy of Mexico without great enthusiasm. But Viceroy Apodaca received it at a time when New Mexico was again seemingly in danger, and he tended to give de Mun's report more credence.

Apodaca's reaction was due in part to the fact that an integral part of the American Indian trade had gone far beyond the pale of settlements, and the United States government, after the War of 1812, endeavored to protect its traders by counteracting foreign intruders and influence. This required the establishment of a military frontier far in advance of the centers of civilization. Part of this program was the so-called Yellowstone expedition of 1818, the first American military movement toward the Northwest. The basic scope of policy, and of that expedition, included removal of British traders from United States territory and counteraction of British influence over the Indian tribes. The expedition was also to establish a military post at the mouth of the Minnesota River, a post among the Mandan Indians, and later, forts on the Yellowstone River. A fort was established at Council Bluffs from which the projected plan might be carried out. It was widely advertised and much was expected from it: the securing of the West, elimination of British traders, collection of geographical knowledge, promotion of western immigration, protection and stimulation of the fur trade, and establishment of communications with the Pacific. In addition to these admitted aims, the Spaniards suspected another: the American invasion of New Mexico. An advance contingent under Talbot Chambers started out in 1818. Manuel Lisa, having gone ahead, ascended the Missouri to prepare the Indians for the coming of American troops.

Spanish consular agents in St. Louis and New Orleans kept the minister in Washington and frontier officials informed of the progress of the expedition. The fact that Manuel Lisa had been sent ahead prompted particular suspicion since he was an experienced mountain man and Indian trader, knew the routes, and was Spanish. In fact, he might have been the principal cause of Spanish fear that the expedition was a threat to New Mexico. Moreover, a newspaper account stated that a branch of the Yellowstone, the Bighorn, was navigable within New Mexico.

Spanish reaction was forthcoming. Spanish Consul Felipe Fatio at New Orleans informed both Onís and Viceroy Apodaca that the American expedition constituted a definite threat to the frontiers of New Mexico. The viceroy passed this information on to Antonio Cordero y Bustamante, acting commandant general of the Provincias Internas, but neither Cordero nor Apodaca could locate the Yellowstone River on any available maps. They did, however, believe that it apparently had its source in New Mexico. Melgares himself undertook a comprehensive investigation of the Yellowstone, which he estimated to be three hundred leages north of Santa Fe, farther even than St. Louis. He correctly surmised that the purpose of the American expedition was to eliminate the British from the Yellowstone, and expressed doubts that it could successfully attack New Mexico, even if it had that goal, due to intervening deserts and mountains. It would, however, be some time before Melgares could verify the presence of the American expedition on the Yellowstone because of the snow which blocked the mountain passes to the north. He offered, however, to expel the Americans. Melgares also suggested working with the British, whom he felt would probably cooperate because of their threatened interests. Here again were the same ingredients of Spanish borderland conflict that had existed previously in the Mississippi-Upper Missouri valleys. The same ingredients, plans, methods, and motives—only with the major parties, English and Americans, somewhat reversed vis-á-vis the Spaniard—predominated.

Melgares meanwhile prepared New Mexico for a possible American attack. He needed no additional troops, for an arrangement of peace with the Navajo had freed New Mexico's militia to meet the American threat. Veteran troops would garrison the two principal mountain passes in the direction of the Yellowstone and the Arkansas rivers; and the number of Spanish agents among the surrounding Indian tribes was doubled in order to prevent a surprise attack.

In the meantime, the viceroy had received de Mun's report and forwarded it, with recommendations to meet some of the obvious weaknesses outlined in it. Among other things, he strongly urged fortification of the passes, and a typical bureaucrat, requested cost estimates. Responding to the de Mun report, Melgares declared that the three passes were defensible and already fortified. He did, however, point out other avenues of approach open to the

Americans. Moreover, Melgares believed that construction of permanent forts would be costly, and instead recommended the erection of temporary structures which could be readily covered or destroyed. Melgares dispatched full details of his proposals to Cordero, including plans for forts, and details of the costs, at Taos, El Vado, and Ojo Caliente. Taos was considered the most urgent since it would block the closest and best route into New Mexico. The commandant general sent Melgares' report on to the viceroy in Mexico City, who turned over the plans to engineer Juan Sociat. Sociat, however, was disturbed by the paucity of Melgares' information and requested maps of the terrain around the proposed forts, as well as information concerning the most suitable types of fortifications and the kind of garrisons needed. He did, however, urge that orders for materials and equipment for the forts be initiated immediately. These delays, typical in Spanish bureaucracy, occurred even though the viceroy had indicated that the fortification of New Mexico was a matter of great urgency.

The commandant general of the Interior Provinces, meanwhile, was of two minds. On the one hand, he suggested that New Mexico's vulnerability might encourage the Americans to attack, but maintained that the obstacles to such an undertaking, including Spanish influence over the surrounding Indian tribes, made the danger less than might be expected. At the same time, he ordered an expedition into the Yellowstone area with the understanding that no action was to be taken against the Americans. Spanish troops were merely to observe American movements and prevent any attempt by them to enter New Mexico. Upon receiving that information, Melgares sent out a party of fifteen men under Juan Chalvert to the Yellowstone, but they saw no signs of Americans. The same was true of parties traveling over one hundred leagues east of the fortifications at Sangre de Cristo and Cañon de San Fernando. Twenty-four Indians of the "A" (Skiddy-Pawnee) tribe from the vicinity of the Missouri River had arrived in Santa Fe and reported having seen nothing of the Yellowstone expedition. At this point, Melgares concluded that there was no need for further expeditions unless concrete evidence of American presence was received.

Fatio, however, kept Spanish officialdom supplied with alarming reports. It was Spanish Vice-consul Juan Gualbert Ortega, at St. Louis, who kept Fatio informed. Ortega believed strongly that the objective of United States expeditions was the occupation of the

Spanish Provincias Internas, claiming that United States designs on Spanish lands had increased since the signing of the Adams-Onís treaty. Ortega relayed news about a large number of soldiers and steamboats leaving St. Louis, and predicted that Benjamin O'Fallon, the Indian agent for the Missouri who was accompanying the expedition, would probably lead the invasion of New Mexico. American spies were allegedly already scurrying to various points in New Mexico, where they would recruit supporters and lead an attack in cooperation with the main American force on the Yellowstone. Ortega even enclosed newspaper accounts to substantiate his theories. Fatio suggested that immediate, decisive action would offset the American threat.

In October 1819, Melgares received information from mestizo Manuel Antonio Rivera recently arrived in Santa Fe from a trading expedition, which made Fatio's information all the more plausible. Rivera had met some Comanche who informed him that, according to the Jumano, the Americans planned to attack New Mexico from three different directions. Rivera claimed to verify part of this report by indicating that while visiting the Cuampe Indians with his Comanche companions, he had met a party of five Americans and seven Spanish traders under the leadership of two former residents of New Mexico.

Melgares prepared to meet the invasion. He sent Juan Lucero to investigate the presence of foreigners among the surrounding Indian nations, and letters to ascertain the extent of firearms, men, and materials available in New Mexico. Melgares also asked the viceroy for immediate aid and additional soldiers.

Melgares, obviously apprehensive, became thoroughly alarmed when his newly established post at Sangre de Cristo Pass reported that one of his reconnaissance expeditions under José Antonio Valenzuela had been attacked by a force of one hundred Indians. The Indians were repulsed with heavy losses, but at the cost of five Spanish soldiers. The Indians, then, were not all loyal, and Melgares immediately reinforced the Sangre de Cristo garrison. Melgares told García Conde who sent the information on to Apodaca that the attacking Indians were under American influence, indicating that perhaps "the bandits of the infamous Banjamin O'Fallon" were already nearing New Mexico.

The viceroy had always been willing, if necessary, to send aid to Melgares, especially if Rivera's report proved true; but, he maintained, despite Rivera's report that there was no hard evidence of American plans to attack New Mexico. He so informed Commandant General Conde. Since his troops were urgently needed elsewhere, he could not reinforce New Mexico until the need was more obvious. The attack on the Sangre de Cristo garrison, however, convinced Apodaca that the American invasion of New Mexico was imminent. Melgares was ordered to complete the fortifications of Taos, El Vado, and Ojo Caliente, and was informed that some troops destined for Texas were in readiness to send to New Mexico. Apodaca also ordered García Conde to use all men and materials at his command to counter the American threat.

While the higher echelons became increasingly worried, alarm in New Mexico was receding. Again it was a case of distant officials operating with outdated information; talking, but not producing. New Mexico now found little evidence of Americans. Two large parties, reconnoitering on the Platte, returned without any evidence of foreign presence. A second Indian attack on the Sangre de Cristo garrison had been successfully repulsed. Melgares, after reports from his agents among the Indians, was convinced that the attacking Indians were acting independently of the Americans.

Melgares had also become more confident of New Mexico's defensive capabilities—militias had been training on Sundays and four thousand men were ready to confront an invading force. "I have spies and agents among the Kiowa, Comanche, Orejon and other tribes that occupy [the area from] the Missouri to the cordillera of the Sierra that forms a barrier to New Mexico," said Melgares. In fact, Melgares offered to ease both García Conde and Apodaca's minds, and the problem of defense of the Provincias Internas, when he presented an alternate plan to organize and train a force—if the necessary money would be allocated—and keep them in a stage of readiness as long as the American danger existed. Apodaca, still convinced that an attack on New Mexico was very probable, believed that Melgares' conclusions with respect to the attacks on the Sangre de Cristo garrisons had been made too hastily and without sufficient investigation. Apodaca ordered García Conde to instruct Melgares to continue to work on the fortifications, and to remain on the alert for a surprise attack; he rejected Melgares' plan for a more effective New Mexican militia.

By now Lucero had again returned to Santa Fe following a visit to the Plains. He reported that the Comanche had informed him of a party of Jmericans which, though then at some distance from the province, planned to come to New Mexico in the spring to trade with the Spaniards. García Conde tended to doubt the story but ordered Melgares to be vigilant and not allow the Americans to enter New Mexico under any pretext. Apodaca viewed the report with more alarm, and repeated his previous orders about the fortifications. He also ordered García Conde to move his headquarters from Durango to Chihuahua where he might better deal with the threat to New Mexico's borders. Melgares turned out to be right. He was plagued only with chronic Indian troubles. By 1820, the fiasco of the American Yellowstone expedition had come to an end, and in February of that year the alarmist Fatio died. The wasted efforts of two years, on the basis of rumor, suspicion, and innuendo had been costly to the efficient operations of New Mexico. New Mexico was able to turn its attention to more tangible domestic problems. By that time, too, another Spanish borderland had fallen under the United States flag, for the Adams-Onís Treaty of 1819 had established, at least on paper, the western boundary of the Louisiana Purchase.

The encroachments upon Spain's dominions in 1818, had made it a particularly critical year for Spain. The United States held Amelia Island, Andrew Jackson was in Florida, James Long and General Jean Joseph Amable Humbert schemed for Texas, and Benjamin O'Fallon and Talbot Chambers worried New Mexico. There were also filibusters and traders: Jean Lafitte in the Gulf of Mexico and John Downs [Downes] at Acapulco harassed the coasts and the trade of the Spanish empire, and Hippolyte de Bouchard's privateers were off California. From the Yellowstone to the Louisiana-Texas frontier, and from the Gulf of Mexico to the Rocky Mountains (occupying what in general terms may be called the Texas and New Mexico country), the Spanish borderlands—including the last frontier of Spanish Louisiana—were being harassed. The old fears of the dreaded, aggressive Anglo-Americans again plagued the Spanish monarchy, whose mighty empire already was falling throughout the Americas. A weak, paternalistic, and overextended government, high costs, inefficiency, and antiquated methods pitted against the more youthful and driving Americans, had resulted once again in the loss of a borderland area. The aggressive, adventurous, and imaginative Americans, with far more available resources, had planted the Stars and Stripes over new territory. The American explorer and fur trader had pointed the way, and the diplomats had followed, remaking the boundaries—in this case the Adams-Onís Treaty, signed in 1819 with the exchange of ratifications two years later.

The borderlands of New Mexico had once been part of the Spanish claim to all of North America. But by 1819 Spain's empire had been cut back to an area bounded by the Sabine River, the roof of the Rocky Mountains, and the forty-second parallel. The long record of the Spaniards, begun in 1595, came to an end in New Mexico in 1821 with the winning of independence in New Spain. Spanish interests in the borderlands were terminated, or what was left of them, transferred to the independent subjects of Mexico. This coincided with the rise of the Santa Fe trade and trasferred the chronic problem of the Spaniards—defense—to the Mexicans. It was, at best, an ambiguous legacy.

The north-northeastern frontier of the Viceroyalty of New Spain, the last Spanish borderland, and the last frontier of Spanish Louisiana, had stretched northward to varying extent since 1763. But England and American traders had repeatedly parried these northward thrusts. The English pried loose the extreme northeastern corner in time for the Americans to obtain the territory under its flag in 1803. The Spanish frontier defense, after Napoleon's sale of Louisiana to the United States, became startlingly similar to that of the previous period. Spain claimed the Missouri River as its northern boundary and attempted to fortify it to the mountains, and to reinforce its northern boundary across the mountains to the Pacific. This was the ultimate objective of the Spaniards from St. Louis in the latter part of the eighteenth century and early years of the nineteenth century. Cut short by the English in the Nootka Sound controversy on the northwest coast, Spain was pushed further and further southward along the Pacific, effectively to just above San Francisco. Further whittling away at the Spanish borderland near the end of Spanish rule in North America left the boundary in the south at the mouth of the Sabine in the Gulf of Mexico, in the east along the Red and Arkansas rivers to the Rocky Mountains, and in the north along the forty-second parallel to the Pacific Coast.

Just as from 1763 to 1803 the Spanish Illinois Country and Spanish Louisiana were in general considered by the Spaniards to be buffer colonies protecting their more valuable mines of Old Mexico, so, after the Louisiana Purchase, New Mexico and Texas were considered the keys to the more valuable possessions of Spain in North America. In 1812, New Mexico's delegate to the Spanish Cortes, Pedro Bautista de Pino had declared that if the Americans took New Mexico, they would master the other frontier provinces and be in a position to invade the Kingdom of Mexico. In truth, this nearly came about thirty-six years later, when the United States went to war with Mexico, finally wresting control of New Mexico and California in the process. The Spanish Borderland in North America gave way to a borderland between independent Mexico and a United States caught up in a spirit of Manifest Destiny.

Bibliographical Notes

CHAPTER 1
The First Frontier: Along the Mississippi (to 1777)

This chapter has been based on a number of printed works and upon two doctoral dissertations. Of the older and standard histories of Louisiana, the best is still Charles E.A. Gayarré, *History of Louisiana*, 4 vols. (New York: Redfield, 1854-66). Alcée Fortier, *A History of Louisiana*, 4 vols. (Paris: Goupil & Co, 1904) has a short account. A second edition of volume 2 of his work was brought out in 1972 by Jo Ann Carrigan, whose notes and comments occupy the greater half of the volume, making it the most valuable study covering the Spanish period. Of the one-volume histories of Louisiana, that by Edwin Adams Davis, *Louisiana, A Narrative History* (3d. ed., Baton Rouge: Claitor's Publishers, 1969) is the best and contains a very good chapter on Spanish Louisiana. Vincente Rodríguez Casado's *Los primeros años de dominación española en la Luisiana* (Madrid: Consejo Superior de Investigaciones Científicas, Instituto Gonzalo Fernández de Oviedo, 1942) has excellent information on Ulloa, and gives some documentation. John Preston Moore is preparing a biography of Antonio de Ulloa; his "Antonio de Ulloa: A Profile of the First Spanish Governor of Louisiana," appeared in *Louisiana History* 8: 189-218, and his "Anglo Spanish Rivalry on the Louisiana Frontier, 1763-68," in John Francis McDermott, ed., *The Spanish in the Mississippi Valley 1762-1804* (Urbana: University of Illinois Press, 1974), pp. 72-86. Very useful are John W. Caughey, *Bernardo de Gálvez in Louisiana, 1776-1783* (Berkeley: University of California Press, 1934); Clarence E. Carter, *Great Britain and the Illinois Country, 1763-1774* (Washington, D.C.: American Historical Association, 1910); James E. Winston, "Causes and Results of the Revolution of 1768 in Louisiana," *Louisiana Historical Quarterly* 15: 181-213; and Louis Houck, *A History of Missouri from the Earliest Explorations and Settlements until the Admission of the State into the Union*, 3 vols. (Chicago: R.R. Donnelley & Sons, 1908).

David Bjork, "Establishment of Spanish Rule in Louisiana 1762-1770" deals with O'Reilly's regime, and A.P. Nasatir, "Indian Trade and Diplomacy in the Spanish Illinois, 1763-1792" deals with Upper Louisiana. Both are Ph. D. dissertations (University of California, 1923 and 1926 respectively).

Documents are to be found in Louis Houck, *The Spanish Régime in Missouri*, 2 vols. (Chicago: R.R. Donnelley & Sons Co., 1909); Lawrence Kinnaird, *Spain in the Mississippi Valley, 1765-1794*, 3 vols. (Washington, D.C.: U.S. Government Printing Office, 1946-49). See also Herbert E. Bolton, ed. *Athanase de Mézières and the Louisiana-Texas Frontier 1768-1780*, 2 vols. (Cleveland: The Arthur H. Clark Co., 1914); Clarence W. Alvord and Clarence E. Carter's three works, *The Critical Period, 1763-1765, The New Régime, 1765-1767*, and *Trade and Politics, 1767-1769*, all published by the Illinois State Historical Library (Springfield, 1915, 1915, and 1921 respectively); and P. Pittman, *The Present State of the European Settlements on the Mississippi*, ed. by F. Hodder (Cleveland: The Arthur H. Clark Co., 1906). There is a good deal of material in the *Louisiana Historical Quarterly*. Also of value is A.P. Nasatir, "Ducharme's Invasion of Missouri, an Incident in the Anglo-Spanish Rivalry for the Indian Trade of Upper Louisiana," *Missouri Historical Review* 24: 3-25, 238-60, 420-39.

Very useful are Arthur S. Aiton, "The Diplomacy of the Louisiana Cession," *American Historical Review* 36: 701-20; and Baron Marc de Villiers du Terrage, *Les dernières années de la Louisiane française* (Paris: E. Guilmoto, 1904). Recently Professor

J.F. Bannon has summarized and brought up to date bibliographical data relative to Spanish Louisiana in his excellent *The Spanish Borderlands Frontier 1513-1821,* Histories of the American Frontier, ed. by Ray Allen Billington (Albuquerque: University of New Mexico Press, 1974). David K. Texada has summarized the evidence concerning O'Reilly's dealings with the New Orleans rebels in his *Alejandro O'Reilly and the New Orleans Rebels* (Lafayette, La.: University of Southwestern Louisiana, 1970).

CHAPTER 2
The American Revolution and After: The Frontier along the Mississippi

The bibliography of the Frontier and the West during the American Revolutionary period is quite extensive. I have based my account of the time primarily upon my articles "Anglo-Spanish Frontier in the Illinois Country during the American Revolution," *Journal of the Illinois State Historical Society* 21: 3-70, and "St. Louis during the British Attack of 1780," *New Spain and the Anglo-American West,* ed. by Charles W. Hackett, et al., 1:239-61. In addition to the general histories mentioned in Chapter 1, most helpful are John W. Caughey, *Bernardo de Gálvez in Louisiana, 1776-1783* (Berkeley: University of California Press, 1934); James A. James, *The Life of George Rogers Clark* (Chicago: University of Chicago Press, 1928) and *Oliver Pollock: The Life and Times of an Unknown Patriot* (Freeport, N.Y.: Books for Libraries Press, 1970); Lawrence Kinnaird, ed., "Clark-Leyba Papers," *American Historical Review* 41: 92-112; and "The Spanish Expedition against Fort St. Joseph in 1781. A New Interpretation," *Mississippi Valley Historical Review* 19: 173-91; and Joseph P. Donnelly, *Pierre Gibault, Missionary, 1737-1802* (Chicago: Loyola University Press, 1971).

Documentary materials are found in Lawrence Kinnaird, ed., *Spain in the Mississippi Valley, 1765-1794,* 3 vols. (Washington, D.C.: U. S. Government Printing Office, 1946-49); Nasatir, "St. Louis During the British Attack;" James A. James, ed., *George Rogers Clark Papers, 1771-1784,* 2 vols. (Springfield, Ill.: Illinois State Historical Library, 1912, 1926); *Reports of the Canadian Archives,* especially for 1887 which contains a calendar of the Haldimand Papers, some of which are reprinted in the *Michigan Pioneer and Historical Collections* and the *Wisconsin Historical Collections.*

For the period after the American Revolution there is a rather lengthy bibliography of published works among which only a few are mentioned here.

Parts of my account have been based again on my dissertation and on Nasatir, "Anglo-Spanish Frontier in the Illinois Country;" Lawrence Kinnaird, "American Penetration into Spanish Territory 1776-1803," (Ph. D. diss., University of California, 1928).

Among many books, reference should be made to Arthur P. Whitaker, *The Spanish-American Frontier: 1783-1795* (Gloucester, Mass.: Peter Smith, 1962) and *The Mississippi Question, 1795-1803* (New York: D. Appleton-Century Co., Inc., 1934); Caroline M. Burson, *The Stewardship of Don Esteban Miró; 1782-1792* (New Orleans: American Printing Co., Ltd., 1940); Samuel F. Bemis, *Jay's Treaty; A Study in Commerce and Diplomacy* (New Haven: Yale University Press, 1962) and *Pinckney's Treaty; A Study in America's Advantage from Europe's Distress, 1783-1800* (Baltimore: The Johns Hopkins Press, 1926); Louis Houck, *A History of Missouri from the Earliest Explorations and Settlements until the Admission of the State into the Union,* 3 vols. (Chicago: R.R. Donnelley & Sons Co., 1908); Charles E. A. Gayarré, *History of Louisiana,* 4 vols. (New York: Redfield, 1854-66); James Ripley Jacobs, *Tarnished Warrior, Major-General James Wilkinson* (New York: The Macmillan Co., 1938); Arthur

B. Darling, *Our Rising Empire, 1763-1803* (London: Oxford University Press, 1940); James B. Musick, *St. Louis as a Fortified Town* (St. Louis: [Press of R.F. Miller] , 1941); A.P. Nasatir, *Spanish War Vessels on the Mississippi 1792-1796* (New Haven: Yale University Press, 1968); Nasatir and E. R. Liljegren, "Materials Relating to the History of the Mississippi Valley," *Louisiana Historical Quarterly* 21: 5-75; E. R. Liljegren, "Jacobinism in Spanish Louisiana 1792-1797," *Louisiana Historical Quarterly* 22: 46-97; Thomas Robson Hay and M. R. Werner, *The Admirable Trumpeter; a Biography of General James Wilkinson* (Garden City, N.Y.: Doubleday, Doran & Co., Inc., 1941); and Max Savelle, *George Morgan, Colony Builder* (New York: Columbia University Press, 1932).

Documentary materials may be found in Kinnaird, ed., *Spain in the Mississippi Valley;* Louis Houck, *The Spanish Régime in Missouri,* 2 vols. (Chicago: R. R. Donnelley & Sons Co., 1909); Manuel Serrano y Sanz, ed., *Documentos históricos de la Florida y la Luisiana, siglos xvi-xvii* (Madrid: V. Suárez, 1912); John W. Caughey, *McGillivray of the Creeks* (Norman: University of Oklahoma Press, 1938); Arthur P. Whitaker, tr. and ed., *Documents Relating to the Commercial Policy of Spain in the Floridas, with incidental reference to Louisiana* (Deland, Fla.: The Florida State Historical Society, 1931); J. A. Robertson, *Louisiana Under the Rule of Spain, France, and the United States, 1785-1807,* 2 vols. (Cleveland: The Arthur H. Clark Co., 1911); Ernest A. Cruikshank, ed., *The Correspondence of Lieut. Governor John Graves Simcoe,* 5 vols. (Toronto: The [Ontario Historical] Society, 1923-26); William Henry Smith, *The St. Clair Papers,* 2 vols. (Cincinnati: R. Clark, 1882); and the *Reports of the Canadian Archives, Wisconsin Historical Collections,* and the *Michigan Pioneer and Historical Collections.*

See also Wayne E. Stevens, *The Northwest Fur Trade, 1763-1800* (Urbana: University of Illinois Press, 1928); Louise Phelps Kellogg, *The British Régime in Wisconsin and the Northwest* (Madison: State Historical Society of Wisconsin, 1935); and Donnelly, *Pierre Gibault.*

CHAPTER 3
Before Zebulon Montgomery Pike: The Frontier on the Upper Mississippi during the later years of Spanish Rule

This chapter is based entirely upon my own research. A volume tentatively entitled *Before Zebulon Montgomery Pike* has recently been completed. Some of the material used appeared in my *Spanish War Vessels on the Mississippi 1792-1796* (New Haven: Yale University Press, 1968). I have also published several articles on the subject, among which may be mentioned "The Anglo-Spanish Frontier on the Upper Mississippi 1786-1796," and "Anglo-Spanish Rivalry in the Iowa Country, 1797-1798," both in the *Iowa Journal of History and Politics* (29: 155-232; 28:337-89). The latter contains a number of documents in translation.

Some documentary publications include: Ernest A. Cruikshank, ed., *The Correspondence of Lieut. Governor John Graves Simcoe,* 5 vols. (Toronto: the [Ontario Historical] Society, 1923-26) and by the same editor, *The Correspondence of the Honorable Peter Russell,* 3 vols. (Toronto: The Ontario Historical Society, 1932);.

Good secondary works are Wayne E. Stevens, *The Northwest Fur Trade, 1763-1800* (Urbana: University of Illinois Press, 1928); Louise Phelps Kellogg, *The British Régime in Wisconsin and the Northwest* (Madison: State Historical Society of Wisconsin, 1935); and Arthur B. Darling, *Our Rising Empire, 1763-1803* (London: Oxford University Press, 1940). Much original documentary material is printed in the *Reports of the Canadian Archives* and the *Michigan Pioneer and Historical Collections.*

CHAPTER 4
Before Lewis and Clark: The Frontier along the Missouri

This chapter is based on my *Before Lewis and Clark. Documents Illustrating the History of the Missouri 1785-1804*, 2 vols. (St. Louis: St. Louis Historical Documents Foundation, 1952). The introduction to that work gives a summary, and the bulk of the two volumes is made up of documents, chiefly from archival sources, dating from 1785 to about 1805. I have published a number of articles on this period, most of which are cited in the above work. Since that work appeared, I have written revised and updated biographical sketches of D'Eglise, Clamorgan, Truteau, Mackay, and Evans, which appeared in LeRoy R. Hafen, ed., *The Mountain Men and the Fur Trade of the Far West*, 10 vols. (Glendale, Ca.: The Arthur H. Clark, Co., 1965-72). For additional materials, see Noel M. Loomis and A. P. Nasatir, *Pedro Vial and the Roads to Santa Fe* (Norman: University of Oklahoma Press, 1967).

CHAPTER 5
The Road to Santa Fe: Genesis of the Santa Fe Trail

This chapter is based chiefly on Noel M. Loomis and A. P. Nasatir, *Pedro Vial and the Roads to Santa Fe* (Norman: University of Oklahoma Press, 1967). Therein will be found, as well as in A. P. Nasatir, *Before Lewis and Clark. Documents Illustrating the History of the Missouri 1785-1804*, 2 vols. (St. Louis: St. Louis Historical Documents Foundation, 1952), the basic materials, in full or in part, and full citations. See also, A. P. Nasatir, "More on Pedro Vial in Upper Louisiana," in John Francis McDermott, ed., *The Spanish in the Mississippi Valley 1762-1804* (Urbana: University of Illinois Press, 1974), pp. 100-119.

CHAPTER 6
On the Road to Texas: The Louisiana-Texas Frontier

There is an increasingly large body of published materials on these aspects of the frontier. No attempt is here made to give a full bibliography; only a few selected items are mentioned. Basic secondary materials include M. A. Hatcher, *The Opening of Texas to Foreign Settlement, 1801-1821* (Austin: University of Texas Press, 1927); Isaac J. Cox, "The Louisiana-Texas Frontier," *Texas State Historical Quarterly* 10: 1-75, and *Southwestern Historical Quarterly* 17: 1-42, 140-87. Cox has written several pertinent articles, as well as a book, *The Early Explorations of Louisiana*, University Studies, Series 2, vol. 2 (Cincinnati: University of Cincinnati Press, 1906). See also Noel M. Loomis and A. P. Nasatir, *Pedro Vial and the Roads to Santa Fe* (Norman: University of Oklahoma Press, 1967) and J. Rydjord, *Foreign Interest in the Independence of New Spain; an Introduction to the War for Independence* (Durham, N.C.: Duke University Press, 1935). Carlos E. Castañeda, *Our Catholic Heritage in Texas, 1519-1936*, 7 vols. (Austin: Von Boeckmann-Jones Co., 1936-58) is a monumental summary and together with Herbert E. Bolton, *Texas in the Middle Eighteenth Century; Studies in Spanish Colonial History and Administration* (New York: Russell & Russell, 1962) provides the best history of Texas. Other good works include Julia K. Garrett, *Green Flag over Texas; a Story of the Last Years of Spain in Texas* (New York: The Cordova Press, Inc., 1939); Harris G. Warren, *The Sword was their Passport: a History of American Filibustering in the Mexican Revolution* (Baton Rouge: Louisiana State University Press, 1943); Henri Folmer, *Franco-Spanish Rivalry in North America,*

1524-1763 (Glendale, Ca.: The Arthur H. Clark Co., 1953); Rupert N. Richardson, *The Comanche Barrier to South Plains Settlement* (Glendale, Ca.: The Arthur H. Clark Co., 1933); Max L. Moorhead, *The Apache Frontier: Jacobo Ugarte and Spanish-Indian Relations in Northern New Spain, 1769-1791* (Norman: University of Oklahoma Press, 1968); John W. Caughey, *Bernardo de Gálvez in Louisiana, 1776-1783* (Berkeley: University of California Press, 1934); Odie B. Faulk, *The Last Years of Spanish Texas, 1778-1821* (The Hague: Mouton, 1964); Lillian E. Fisher, *The Background of the Revolution for Mexican Independence* (Boston: The Christopher Publishing House, 1934); Lawrence Kinnaird, "American Penetration into Spanish Territory 1776-1803" (Ph. D. diss., University of California, 1928); J. Villasana Haggard, "The Neutral Ground between Louisiana and Texas, 1806-1821," *Louisiana Historical Quarterly* 28: 1001-128; and Felix D. Almaraz, Jr. *Tragic Cavalier: Governor Manuel Salcedo of Texas, 1808-1813* (Austin: University of Texas Press, 1971).

For diplomatic history, see Philip C. Brooks, *Diplomacy and the Borderlands; the Adams-Onís Treaty of 1819* (Berkeley: University of California Press, 1939); and Thomas M. Marshall, *A History of the Western Boundary of the Louisiana Purchase, 1819-1841* (Berkeley: University of California Press, 1914).

The most recent account which contains an up-to-date bibliography is John Francis Bannon, *The Spanish Borderlands Frontier 1513-1821,* Histories of the American Frontier, ed. by Ray Allen Billington (Albuquerque: University of New Mexico Press, 1974).

For some documentary publications, see Dunbar Rowland, ed., *Official Letterbooks of W. C. C. Claiborne, 1801-1816,* 6 vols, (Jackson, Miss.: State Department of Archives and History, 1917); Herbert E. Bolton, ed., *Athanase de Mézières and the Louisiana-Texas Frontier, 1768-1780,* 2 vols. (Cleveland: The Arthur H. Clark Co., 1914); C. W. Hackett, ed., *Pichardo's Treatise on the Limits of Louisiana and Texas,* 4 vols. (Austin: University of Texas Press, 1931-46); Lawrence Kinnaird, ed. and tr., *Spain in the Mississippi Valley, 1765-1794,* 3 vols. (Washington, D. C.: U. S. Government Printing Office, 1946-49); J. A. Robertson, *Louisiana under the Rule of Spain, France, and the United States, 1785-1807,* 2 vols. (Cleveland: The Arthur H. Clark Co., 1911); Loomis and Nasatir, *Pedro Vial;* and the three books by Alfred B. Thomas, ed. and tr., *Forgotten Frontiers* (Norman: University of Oklahoma Press, 1932); ed. and tr., *Teodoro de Croix and the Northern Frontier of New Spain* (Norman: University of Oklahoma Press, 1941); and *The Plains Indians and New Mexico, 1751-1778* (Albuquerque: University of New Mexico Press, 1940). Both the *Southwestern Historical Quarterly* and the *Louisiana Historical Quarterly* have a good deal of material on the phases of the Spanish Louisiana frontier discussed in this chapter.

CHAPTER 7
The Last Frontier of Spanish Louisiana: North From Santa Fe

This chapter has been based largely on materials which I found and collected from the archives of New Mexico, Mexico, and Seville. Some of my former students have written theses and dissertations under my direction from this collection of material. Of those, I mention here Donald A. Nuttall, "The American Threat to New Mexico, 1804-1822," (Master's thesis, San Diego State College, 1959) and Ramón Eduardo Ruiz, "For God and Country, the Northeast Frontier of New Mexico to 1820" (Master's thesis, Claremont Graduate School, 1948). There are only a few published materials: Noel Loomis and A.P. Nasatir, *Pedro Vial and the Roads to Santa Fe* (Norman: University of Oklahoma Press, 1967) contains a good deal of material and some published documentation, as does A.P. Nasatir, ed., *Before Lewis and Clark.*

Documents Illustrating the History of the Missouri 1785-1804, 2 vols. (St. Louis: St. Louis Historical Documents Foundation, 1952). See also Lansing B. Bloom, "The Death of Jacques D'Eglise," *New Mexico Historical Review* 2: 369-79; Alfred B. Thomas, "The Yellowstone, James Long, and Spanish Reaction to American Intrusion into Spanish Dominions, 1818-1819," *New Mexico Historical Review* 4: 164-86, and by the same author, "Documents Bearing upon the Northern Frontier of New Mexico, 1818-1819," *New Mexico Historical Review* 4: 146-64. Other scattered documents have also been published. I have added some to the Lisa story in W.B. Douglas, *Manuel Lisa*, ed. by A.P. Nasatir (New York: Argosy-Antiquarian, 1964). Rueben Gold Thwaites, ed., *Original Journals of the Lewis and Clark Expedition, 1804-1806*, 8 vols. (New York: Dodd, Mead, 1904); Elliot Coues, ed., *The Expeditions of Zebulon Montgomery Pike*, 3 vols. (New York: Francis P. Harper, 1895); Donald Dean Jackson, ed., *Letters of the Lewis and Clark Expedition, with Related Documents, 1783-1854* (Urbana: University of Illinois Press, 1962); Donald Dean Jackson, ed., *Zebulon Montgomery Pike, 1779-1813. Jouranls, with Letters and Related Documents* (Norman: University of Oklahoma Press, 1966); Thomas James, *Three Years Among the Indians and Mexicans*, ed. by Walter B. Douglas (St. Louis: Missouri Historical Society, 1916) and of the same book a new edition with an introduction by A.P. Nasatir (Philadelphia: J. B. Lippincott Company, 1962); and J.A. Robertson, *Louisiana Under the Rule of Spain, France, and the United States, 1785-1807*, 2 vols. (Cleveland: The Arthur H. Clark Co., 1911) are all useful and important.

Helpful secondary materials include L. Navarro García, *Las provincias internas en el siglo xix* (Sevilla: Escuela de Estudios Hispano-Americanos, 1965); Charles L. Kenner, *A History of New Mexican-Plains Indians Relations* (Norman: University of Oklahoma Press, 1969); Isaac J. Cox, "Opening the Santa Fe Trail" *Missouri Historical Review* 25: 30-66; Isaac J. Cox, *The Early Explorations of Louisiana*, University Studies, Series 2, vol. 2 (Cincinnati: University of Cincinnati Press, 1906); and Philip C. Brooks, *Diplomacy and the Borderlands; the Adams-Onís Treaty of 1819* (Berkeley: University of California Press, 1939).

A number of important, related articles have appeared in the *Bulletin* of the Missouri Historical Society, the *Missouri Historical Review*, and the *New Mexico Historical Review*.

Index